Words from the Heart,
Thoughts for the Soul

John J. Chapin

2002

ISBN 0-9719684-0-3

1 2 3 4 5 6 7 8 9
First printing 2002
Printed in Canada

Title: David R. Eid
Cover Design: John Chapin
Art work: Simon Shendelman
Consultant: Keith Mooradian
Format and Layout: Jennifer Brown, Opaque Print Production

For more information: e-mail JCHBruin@aol.com

THIS BOOK IS DEDICATED TO MY PARENTS
ROBERT AND SHIRLEY CHAPIN,
AND MY SISTERS
NANCY AND JEAN MARIE,
WHO HAVE SHOWN ME THE MEANING OF THE WORDS:
LOVE,
LIFE,
COMMITMENT AND MOST IMPORTANT—
FAMILY.

C O N T E N T S _____

INTRODUCTION _____

So many of us get caught up in the habitual trap of living day-to-day. We wake one day, thirty or forty years down the road, to find that almost our whole life is behind us and we haven't become one-tenth of the person we thought we could. We may also face the challenge of keeping our priorities straight and remembering what and who are really important in our lives. It is my desire that some of the following writings will cause you to look at the "Big Picture" instead of getting caught up in life's daily routine.

Some of the poems and essays which follow may inspire, others may open your eyes, and still others may teach you something. Yet, whether you agree or disagree with the message, their objective is the same: To remind you of what's really important, remind you of some of your dreams from the past, and hopefully give you some guidance and inspiration to chase some of your dreams once again.

No one that has walked the planet previously has been exactly like you and no one ever will be. We all are here for a special reason. We all have our place in this world no matter how large or how small. Two beliefs which I hope you will choose to adopt are: One—We only seem to be truly happy when we are part of a team, growing and becoming more, and Two—It's never too late to dream and fulfill our purpose in this world.

At the very least, it is my hope that you are touched in a positive way by this book so that you can have a positive impact on the lives of others around you.

Best Regards and Good Luck,

John J. Chapin

SECTION I

OBSERVATIONS AND ADVICE ABOUT LIFE

GETTING BACK UP_____

One of the most difficult things is to get up after being defeated,
When our physical, emotional and spiritual resources are depleted,

Yet, getting back on our feet is absolutely what we must do,
The pain will ease much quicker than if we sit and stew,

Making that move isn't easy, it's difficult at first,
It's not usually a subject at which we're well versed,

And the more you bounce back, the easier it will get,
On every occasion you'll spend less time with pain and regret,

It's also a good idea to talk to people close to you,
They'll be understanding and help you make it through,

The person you'll become will be well worth the fight,
It will set your mental and emotional well-being right,

Your self-esteem and confidence will begin to thrive,
You'll be joyous for simply the gift of being alive,

And if you slip as you rise, pay it no mind,
Eventually sure footing you're likely to find,

The key isn't how many times you fall to the terrain,
What's important is how many times your stance you regain,

For the winners are the ones that continue to pick themselves up off
   the ground,
And the ones who have risen just one more time than they've fallen
   down.

DEALING WITH LIFE _____

There are times when unexpected situations will come up in our
     lives,
No matter how much we prepare they'll still manage to arise,

Understand that as you go through life these events will occur,
They can put us in a tailspin and cause quite a stir,

Yet they'll effect you the least if you know who you are,
Strong morals, values, and convictions will carry you far,

It's also important to have a support group that's strong,
They'll be there to pick up the pieces whether you're right or you're
     wrong,

Also realize you're human and can't be perfect all the time,
Carry a faith and belief that everything will be fine,

It's also helpful to believe things happen for the best,
This will help you uncover some positives in your difficult test,

And the same is also true when things are going quite well,
Don't lose your perspective and let your head swell,

In the ups and the downs you must keep an even keel,
If you control your emotions, your success you will seal,

So approach life as entertainment pursuing ventures with passion,
And deal with victory and defeat in an elegant fashion,

If you treat life this way it will be one of adventurous fun,
Life is a game with obstacles, yet it's meant to be won.

I've Got a Story to Tell _____

As you go through life and start to figure it out,
You finally see enough and that little voice starts to shout,

The visions in your gut start to become crystal clear,
Your ability to see the world starts to shift into high gear,

Yes by the time you're 30, you have a story,
Plenty of experiences to tell, both of defeat and of glory,

You've seen death and destruction and your own share of pain,
You've seen weddings and births and pleasures to help you sustain,

You've probably loved a time or two and experienced much written
    and spoken,
You may have lived some of life's greatest victories and even had
    your heart broken,

You've learned something about aging and much about your own
    body,
You may even notice some things starting to operate a little shoddy,

You've experienced enough with people and family to know a true
    friend,
You've started to establish those close to you that will be there until
    the end,

Yes, there's nothing like life's experiences and their contribution to
    learning,
The lessons make you wise and a little more discerning,

So experience as much of life as possible with open eyes and open
    mind,
The more life you live with a positive attitude, the more treasures
    you'll find.

Today Is A Special Occasion_____

We all have things we're saving for a special occasion,
The event could be a marriage, first house, or that dream vacation,

We keep it in a drawer or cupboard packed neatly away,
Then we sit back and wait for the arrival of that extraordinary day,

It could be a fancy candle, a bottle, or some clothes we'll wear,
Whatever it is, we stow it away and don't give it another care,

However, if we're not careful, too many years pass us by,
And hidden away that special possession still does lie,

Then others find it going through our effects once we're gone,
What was meant to be used in our lifetime we never did dawn,

Live today as a special occasion because it's all that you've got,
For what tomorrow has in store for us we surely know not,

With your possessions use your head and be intelligent still,
Yet, don't save something not meant to be found in your will,

Your special possessions were meant to be enjoyed and exhibited,
Unveil them and don't be afraid to act a little uninhibited,

Live well now, use your best china, silver and drink your finest
    wine,
And make sure they're not untouched when you cross that Heavenly
    Line.

THE GAMBLER ———————————————

I've watched many a gambler and the result is always the same,
Their life is stolen by a sickness they're unable to tame,

Yes, but I've won big before, is the battle cry they use to continue,
The ultimate outcome of losing they never seem to construe,

They carry on with passion, sure that things will come out a
different way,
Common sense is unable to make those thoughts sway,

They walk into grand places and see what their losing has built,
They risk their life savings and wallow little in guilt,

When ahead it's never enough, the gambler always wants more,
They recover too easily from losing, they pull themselves from the
floor,

They don't see gambling as fun, they see it as a living,
Nothing short of all their money, they end up giving,

They think they'll defy all the odds, they're different from the rest,
Then they end up losing, in spite of their best,

They think they'll make lots of money, the free lunch they're after,
And their life continues, as usual, to be a disaster,

They've done the same exact thing for years and the same results
they get,
Against all odds, on the most ridiculous thing, they're willing to bet,

They can't walk away, surely they'll win the next hand,
If you play long enough, on the down side you'll always land,

So remember, a wealthy gambler is a very cruel joke,
For the professional gambler always dies broke.

THINK _____

We all have a powerful tool that can answer any question,
Yet of everything we have, it tends to be a little used possession,

This tool is our brain, it's said the percentage we use is about five,
It's so powerful it will bring any vision we can imagine alive,

Yet we get caught up in everyday things, it's power we squander,
It'll get us anything we want, if on the big picture we'll ponder,

It has created each great breakthrough and every invention,
It's waiting for us to put it to use toward any intention,

It seems many of us get in a place where we use our brain less,
We take the path of least resistance which leaves us short of
      our best,

Using our brain requires effort, it can indeed be hard work,
Most of us want to avoid that, it's a funny human quirk,

We'd rather go through our lives suffering than face the strange,
No matter how miserable, we desire consistency, we don't want
      to face change,

So we get caught up doing the same things day in and day out,
Then we run on autopilot filled with fear and self-doubt,

Don't make that mistake, have your life follow an adventurous
      course,
Unleash the power of your brain, your most valuable resource.

COMEBACKS _____

As we climb the ladder to eventual success,
Occasionally we hit a bump and we start to regress,

If that downward trend continues too long,
Eventually we may find almost all of our life has gone wrong,

When this happens, hopefully we wake up one day and realize it's
    gone too far,
We notice all of our past success is now a distant star,

We must focus ourselves to get back where we were,
For our recent defeats there's a definite cure,

It's to go back to work and be hungry again,
To turn your dedication from a one to a ten,

The reassuring thing is that you've been at the top before,
So you know you have what you need inside to do it once more,

Just remember what it was like to get to the top the first time,
Then develop some urgency as if your life's on the line,

Create a plan with goals and work hard on it each day,
Then when you're done for today, get some of tomorrow's work
    out of the way,

With determination and dedication you'll get back to first place,
And the person you've become in the victory will show on
    your face,

Just remember this time not to let all that success go,
Don't celebrate too much, make sure you stay in the flow,

Balance your life now that you're back on top of the heap,
Comebacks are possible but not something you want to
    constantly repeat,

It is possible to be number one at work and have all the rest,
Yes, it's challenging and that's what will make you your best.

COMPETITION_____

Competition is something we learn while we're quite young,
It helps shape our character and determine what we'll become,

It teaches us how to win and lose with grace,
There are many emotions it causes us to face,

It makes us work harder at every endeavor,
It forces us to refine our skills and always get better,

It makes sure we're not complacent but rather always push on,
It keeps us up late and gets us up before dawn,

It brings us together and teaches us to work as a team,
And try harder no matter how trivial the job may seem,

It gives us a goal and a purpose to pursue,
It puts us on target and carries us through,

It's a challenge to win, it gives us some fire,
It keeps us going even though we may tire,

It makes sure most stay honest in plying their trade,
If they fail to do so they quickly fade,

It requires companies to provide the consumer with more,
It makes them put a better product in the store,

Competition inspires us to be all we can be,
It takes us to places we thought we'd never see,

We can be anything we want with enough motivation,
Use competition to help spur its creation,

For there's nothing like a good challenge to push you ahead,
Without competition your drive would be dead,

So welcome the competition, work hard and prepare on your part,
You can almost always win, if you've got enough heart.

CHILDREN AND COMPETITION

They talk of not keeping score at children's events,
For self-esteem and dignity they think it prevents,

The competition seems a bit cruel,
We don't want the loser feeling a fool,

No one wants to have children's frail egos marred,
A loss may be the same as being feathered and tarred,

We don't want anyone feeling better or worse than another,
We want everyone the same, individualism we must smother,

Oh sure they may run into it down the road,
By then they'll be more able to handle the load,

With no previous experience, will they figure it out?
Maybe they'll yell and scream a little, or, maybe they'll pout,

Yes, sooner or later the truth they'll perceive,
When 50 show up for a job only one can receive,

In the mean time, we must protect them from competitive pain,
We'll put forth measures that will MAKE them abstain,

Anything where there may be an inkling of competition,
    we'll prevent,
There will be no more dodge ball, tag, or any sporting event,

We'll make sure they play alone and in school are not scored,
We'll keep their world protected from pain and discord,

We'll let the real world and truth hit all at once,
And ultimately have ourselves to blame for being the dunce,

On second thought, let's give children credit and let them live
    some of life,
There's a happy medium between too much protection and
    too much strife,

A little competition is good supervised in the right way,
Our children will be more well rounded at the end of the day,

For competition is healthy and helps to bring out our best,
Occasionally it's good to have to pass some sort of test.

CONCENTRATION _____

There's an idea that can get you to your destination faster
    than all others,
It's a principle by which the universe governs,

It's the focus of concentration on one idea at a time,
Turn it to a single area of life and you're sure to make it shine,

It will cut through, clarify and take clouded vision away,
It will keep you on track and focused on your goal throughout
    the day,

In an area of interest, it will allow you to make extraordinary gains,
It will help you get there faster and minimize pains,

Like sunbeams through a magnifying glass, it's power is mighty,
It will prevent you from ideas that are vague or even a bit flighty,

You'll spend much less time on a project than you have in the past,
When you see the results, your motivation will last,

Concentration will bring all your focus to bear,
You'll suddenly realize you have ability that's tough to compare,

You can't focus on two things at the same time and have any success,
If you stay on that course, both areas will regress,

So choose one task at a time and give it all you've got,
With concentration and focus you've got your best shot.

COOPERATION

Occasionally in this world we need others to help us get by,
We can't make it totally alone no matter how hard we try,

Through the spirit of cooperation we get what we need,
It's off of bonding and togetherness that this ideal does feed,

If we work collectively as a team to achieve what we desire,
We'll find it's easy to light the flame of that emotional fire,

For we need to be part of something bigger than us,
To give and take with others is an absolute must,

A strong support group will give us strength when we're down,
They'll remind us of our importance and help us turn it around,

Yes our ability to get along with others and interact is the key,
Only when at peace with those important to us are we totally free,

Much of life depends on how well people like us and we in
    turn them,
From our relationships either turmoil or happiness stem,

We must learn to live well with others and treat them with respect,
If we do this skillfully, an abundant life and happiness we should
    fully expect.

ACTION—REACTION

Many people wait for others to move to them before they
    will budge,
Yet often, if we move first, we'll find people only need a
    little nudge,

They may be looking at us and reacting to what they think they see,
We may want to meet them, yet our lack of action deafens that plea,

It's like sitting at the fire waiting for heat before we put in wood,
If no one wants to make the first move, maybe we should,

In this world we can't always expect others to come to our door,
Many times we must go to them, though it may be a difficult chore,

If the world is to be a better place, why not let it start where
    you are,
If you reach out to many others you'll tend to travel quite far,

Don't stay in your house and let people guess what your thinking,
Go out and meet them, talk to them and remove any inkling,

For you'll find most people friendly and willing to converse,
Yet if you stay inside with the door closed it will be much the
    reverse,

People will reflect back to you the action you show,
From their reaction to you, your reputation you'll know,

So approach people with a smile and good cheer, make the
    first move,
Soon you'll make friends without even thinking and you'll be
    in the groove.

DEATH ─────────────────────────────────────

Death, the mere word strikes fear into many of us,
It's a subject that countless don't even like to discuss,

I guess I can't blame them, for its consequences are very mysterious,
The different viewpoints on its meaning can leave us quite delirious,

Some see its inevitable grip as an end, a final destination,
I prefer to think of it as our soul simply bringing another
    chapter to culmination,

Have you ever known another that has significantly impacted
    the world,
That through them and their words and actions, amazing events
    unfurled,

When you think of that person and all their vigor and drive,
It's hard to picture that spirit no longer alive,

Surely that life must go somewhere, all that energy cannot just
    be gone,
Yes our body is no longer full of life, but certainly, our spirit
    lives on,

And how about all the miracles and stories of haunted places,
I'd swear I've seen God in generous human feats and several
    people's faces,

Then there's our Western Calendar, its year based upon the
    birth of God's son,
Undoubtedly the event had a huge impact for that to have
    been done,

There's the belief of billions and the wonder of life on the planet
    which we occupy,
Can that many people be wrong, could all this life just possibly die,

How did this complex world get started, could these amazing things

just evolve,
I believe it's impossible that around a higher force this incredible
plan doesn't revolve,

So yes, death is still a mystery and it will remain so until that bridge
we cross,
Yet while my body is under it, I'm betting my spirit will be looking
down upon the moss.

FACING DEATH_____

Facing Death is an experience so uncertain,
Do we view it as a new beginning or, indeed the final curtain,

It's funny that we avoid so many things we fear each day,
Yet death is one event from which we cannot sway,

It is said there are no guarantees but taxes and death,
Yet truly, the only promise is our physical body's final breath,

The clarity an approaching death can give us is second to none,
Some find God, some find family and others wish they'd had
    more fun,

We all face it, from the mightiest of warriors to the meekest
    among us,
Some are scared while others seem to find a calming trust,

Yes surely the grip of death we will one day know,
Yet will our soul be prepared at the time we go,

We must let anger, resentment, and other ugly emotions depart,
This is only the beginning, but a very good start,

We must forgive others and be at peace with our world,
It's important that all our being's dark places are unfurled,

All the rooms of our soul must be open and filled with light,
Into the deepest depths of our person it's necessary to have
    clear sight,

We must be running the show and be dominant in our personal
    realm,
It's essential to be completely alert and all knowing at the helm,

Once you have achieved this state, you'll find your mind and soul
    are eased,
And you'll bathe in joyous peace of mind as your soul from your
    body is released.

PASSION ─────────────────────────────

Nothing great can be accomplished without great will and desire,
Passion is the label that most give to this ultimate fire,

It's a flame that burns deep inside us, almost out of control,
It engulfs our whole being, our heart, mind, and soul,

It wakes us early in the morning and keeps us up well into night,
It seems to keep us going forever and fills us with plenty of fight,

It is something larger than us, yet defines who we are,
If we point it in the right direction, it will surely take us far,

It defines our highest values and ideals and makes them one,
Though difficult and challenging, those immersed call it fun,

It pushes us to greater heights and makes us better than yesterday,
It reminds us what's most important and guides us along the way,

It drives us to create something that will be here long after
　　we're gone,
Its vision is clear to us immediately as it wakes us before the dawn,

Passion gives our life meaning, it puts purpose in our walk,
It spurs us on to action as opposed to empty talk,

To live a full life you need a passion for which you'll gladly die,
With enough motivation and reasons why, your limit is the sky.

DETERMINATION ————————————————

Determination is the measure of our desire to win,
It dictates whether difficulties inspire us or wear our hearts thin,

Probably the most important factor in determination is why,
The more powerful our reasons are, the harder we'll try,

Strong determination seems to overcome obstacles of the past,
Through almost any difficulty or setback our drive seems to last,

If previously we've lacked self confidence or the knowledge
    we need,
Determination seems to defeat these and bring our resources
    up-to-speed,

It is a major factor in our winning or losing,
And its level is up to us for the choosing,

You have to come up with great reasons why you MUST reach
    your goal,
Then you have to decide that you're willing to pay any toll,

It's important to constantly remind yourself of why this goal is key,
Before it's actually achieved, in your mind's eye you must see,

Decide you will not give up without a most valiant fight,
Concentrate single-mindedly and soon you'll see the light,

Act as if there's no way your objective will fail,
Then work mightily on every single detail,

And your determination will take on a life of its own,
It will transform your world, you'll speak with a different tone,

Go forth and conquer any quest you've ever dared to conceive,
With enough determination, any vision you've ever dreamed of
    you can achieve.

EXPANDING OUR HORIZONS _____

Most of us live day-to-day in our own little world,
There's so much of life we leave completely unfurled,

We stay in our small universe and don't wander out much,
With ninety-percent of the planet, we're completely out of touch,

We think we have all the information we need and thus no
    longer grow,
We make decisions and judgments based upon the little we know,

Because most of our activities are always the same,
It's difficult for us to expand our mind frame,

Then when we have trouble seeing another's view,
We never stop to think maybe our vision's askew,

When we do something different it expands our gaze,
We're able to grasp more, we're in less of a haze,

The more we experience, the more we tend to open our mind,
Suddenly the answers to difficult questions are easy to find,

We should try many things out of our standard domain,
Otherwise relatively ignorant we're sure to remain,

So live more of life and what it has to submit,
And you'll find you're a happier person and much more mentally fit.

Finding God_____

Some of us are born with God and Religion and some are not,
Some are outward with their beliefs and they're easy to spot,

Some learn about God and Religion and carry it until they die,
Others do or don't learn, but either way they take a bye,

It's still interesting to study those that do find belief,
Some find it without pressure, some find it seeking relief,

I've noticed that people without it many times find it just
    before death,
I've watched death row inmates find it before they take their
    last breath,

Then there are those who need to see nothing, God's presence
    they know,
They go to church and sing proudly, they radiate an eminent glow,

Still others wonder, is there a God, they stop to ponder,
What's out there for us in the after-world yonder,

Whether you will find God or not is a decision only you can make,
You'll decide if Religion is a lifestyle in which you'll partake,

Yet if you're looking, I believe God can be found right where
    you stand,
In watching people helping others and giving them a hand,

It's treating another as we would have them treat us,
It's realizing there are many good people we still can trust,

For God is in each one of us, no matter how small,
He's waiting for us to see him and answer his call,

So if you're looking for God, search for the good in others around,
For in the kindness and mercy of another is where He can be found.

FINDING OUR OWN HAPPINESS_____

I sat and struggled with a difficult decision, surely there must be
a way,
I asked my Dad what he thought, in hopes he'd shed some light
of day,

His answer was quizzical, it seemed to get me no further along,
He told me whatever decision I made, it definitely wouldn't be
wrong,

How could that be I wondered, I was hoping he'd have a more
objective view,
He also said something about each individual seeing their own
situation through,

It wasn't until much later that the meaning of his words actually
crystallized,
Each person must make their own happiness was the truth I finally
realized,

Deep down inside, we know what we can live with and what's right
for each of us,
To make up our own minds and live with that decision is an absolute
must,

For there are many roads before us, any one of which we can take,
Only we can find our own happiness through the decisions we
make.

FORGIVENESS _____

Perhaps one of the most difficult things is to forgive and forget,
Yet if we don't develop the habit, it's us who will live in regret,

By holding a grudge it's not the other person we victimize,
It eats us up inside and leads to our quicker demise,

But how can we forgive someone after what they have done,
It may have hurt deeply, perhaps its effects are hard to shun,

Realize that people do the best with the experiences they own,
Based upon their life, they've simply reaped what they've sown,

They may not understand things as you do, or see the same
     repercussions,
Perhaps you'd be on two different wavelengths when having
     discussions,

Or maybe much time has gone by since that disparaging condition,
Possibly they've changed and now would make a different decision,

And just because you forgive, does not mean you have to be
     vulnerable a second time,
As far as opening your life to that person once again, you don't need
     to cross that line,

You only need to forgive and forget to help yourself to clear things
     inside,
Without the negative feelings, you'll be in for a much easier ride,

That person must live with him or herself and the unfortunate event,
Your only goal is to separate yourself from the situation and let bad
     feelings vent,

So take the weight off your shoulders, move forward and lighten
     your load,
You'll find your life will be much happier and better off down
     the road.

FRAME OF MIND _____

The battle is won or lost before it actually takes place,
Inside ourselves we know the fate we'll eventually face,

We have either prepared and calculated each possible ordeal,
Or we haven't and it's probably defeat we'll eventually feel,

The attitude with which we approach a task is most of the test,
It determines whether we simply go through the motions or give
    it our best,

Because whether you think you can or you can't, your vision is true,
You'll either do half the job, or carry it through,

So before you engage, decide what outcome you desire,
Then work hard and prepare, charge ahead with fire,

Stay positive and upbeat, believe in who you are,
With a good outlook and self-esteem, you're sure to go far,

If you visualize your goal and feel it before it's actually achieved,
The odds will be much more in your favor of it being truly
    perceived,

Work with persistence and determination no matter the chance,
Take pride in the process and celebrate each minor advance,

For the journey to the goal is what will make you a better being,
Your final destination is dependant upon what you're already seeing,

So go ahead with a superior frame of mind and dive right in,
With enough good attitude and conviction, you'll surely win.

Freedom_____

There's an element of our society which most of us simply assume,
It gives us unlimited choices and almost infinite room,

It's the concept of freedom, and its meaning is grand,
It gives us rights and protection wherever we stand,

We go through our day not really appreciating its meaning,
To lose it after all, would be truly demeaning,

We live in the richest populace with more opportunity than ever,
Why some people complain, I'll understand never,

We can think and believe and do what we may,
We can leave its borders or happily stay,

We can surf the net, start our own business or, go anywhere,
We're free to worship or give to any organization we care,

It's something we take for granted because most of us know it
      so well,
Living without freedom is a story the majority cannot tell,

Yet when you see other countries and the overwhelming oppression,
It's easy to see why for them freedom's an obsession,

They can be tortured, imprisoned and pushed for no reason,
War and chaos reign no matter the season,

The water is dirty, their food full of infection,
From most major ailments, they have no protection,

Yes, we are far from that, our world mostly clean and pure,
So if you think you're lucky but, really not sure,

Rest assured that you are, whereas most others in this world are not,
Many have given their lives and others happily would, to have
      what you've got.

FRUSTRATION _____

Frustration seems like an enemy yet it can be our best friend,
If we'll just stop and listen to the message it's trying to send,

The purpose of frustration is to push us to become even more,
To move us out of our comfort zone and make us better than before,

For if we were always content there would be no reason to
    further evolve,
Around the same unchanging experiences our lives would
    always revolve,

Frustration causes us to step out of the norm and learn something
    new,
It makes us study and think each part of the process through,

And if we refuse to heed its warning and do just the same,
It will continue to stay around until it drives us nearly insane,

The first step with frustration is to decide to keep a clear mind,
Then we must search for the solution it's helping us find,

There is always an answer, some kind of way out of this mess,
And we'll grow as a person through this challenging test,

So the next time you feel frustrated get excited instead,
For you're about to grow and move further ahead,

Use frustration as a tool to strengthen your motivation,
And it will spur you to growth beyond your wildest imagination.

HEALTH _____

There are not many possessions more important than health,
Without it, our lives would be meaningless regardless of wealth,

In carrying on with our daily lives it plays such an important role,
A lack of mental and physical health can take quite a toll,

It affects our attitudes and what we can and can't do,
If our health's good, almost anything it will carry us through,

When we feel alive and energetic we think in a positive way,
When the opposite, we tend to have a miserable day,

If our mind is willing, yet the body is weak,
Our reactions will typically be timid and meek,

Our body is the vehicle we need to carry us through the years,
If we don't take care of it, we'll be driven to heartache and tears,

It's as simple as exercising a little in a way that is fun,
Whether it's something in a gymnasium, or out in the sun,

Cardiovascular is by far the most important part,
Twenty minutes, three times a week is great for the heart,

Follow that with strength training three times a week,
And soon you'll find your body operating near peak,

Next, mix in a well-balanced diet with water and food that's good,
If you don't know what to eat, read books to find out what
    you should,

Do what you must to take care of your body, heart, soul and mind,
And an abundance of peace and tranquility you're more than likely
    to find.

HUMAN POTENTIAL _____

What are we really capable of I've often pondered,
What if we used ALL our abilities and nothing was squandered,

To see some of the things mankind has accomplished is truly
    miraculous,
But what about the individual, isn't his or her ability also fabulous,

As a society, we were able to put a man on the moon,
Is an individual capable of a similar tune,

When you look at human potential and all it entails,
It seems a wonder that any of us fails,

It is really true we use such a small percentage of brain,
What if from any limiting beliefs we were to totally refrain,

It's interesting to see people under hypnosis suddenly correct,
Instantly things they weren't good at, they now are perfect,

The ability was there all along, it's simply our state of mind,
If we really believe we can do it, then the power we'll find,

When you look at people over history and what they have done,
It appears as though an individual can do anything under the sun,

It seems our limitations are what we believe our abilities to be,
When we know we can do something, it's fruition we see,

So never say "I can't" and watch negative talk,
If you believe that you can, then you'll walk the walk,

Your potential IS unlimited, you can do MORE than others
    have done,
So plan a challenging life with exciting goals and go have some fun.

IMAGE IS EVERYTHING_____

Like it or not, we live in a society where image is key,
And people judge most often by that which they see,

People will judge you on your weight and the clothes you wear,
They'll look at your jewelry and how you cut your hair,

They'll judge your voice, your car and your house,
They'll assume things about you after seeing your spouse,

That's not to say this dissecting by others is totally fair,
Yet it says why we give our looks and possessions such great care,

The key is not to be so concerned with what others conclude,
The less you care what they think the more scrutiny you'll elude,

Yet if you want to work somewhere or hang in a certain club,
Realize the image that the group is trying to dub,

For having the same outward appearance could take you far,
As long as you're not forgetting the person you really are,

Realize how image works in our society and use it as you will,
And remember if your outward and inward image match, you'll
    be happier still,

The most important issue is how your image makes you feel inside,
For if you're in congruence with that image your life will be a
    great ride.

IN THE EYES OF THE BEHOLDER _____

We all have a self-concept of who we believe ourselves to be,
It's funny to notice an outsider's view and what they actually see,

For more often than not, another's idea of us is more than our view,
We'd swear we could conquer the world if their vision was true,

They tend to see the outside and the positive qualities we possess,
We tend to focus on what goes on inside and the internal mess,

They see a person who seems to have all their ducks in a row,
While we walk around reliving past defeats with their pain still
    in tow,

What if we could see ourselves through the eyes of another being,
More than likely, at that point, the real truth we'd be seeing,

Because it is true that we can all be so much more,
If we'd focus on the positives and let negatives fly out the door,

And what if that vision shows a person you wish you were not,
Then this simple exercise can surely help you a lot,

For it will show you why you constantly face problems in life,
And why your relationships are always filled with much strife,

Either way, you will find another's view of you an eye-opening
    event,
For it can give you something to live up to or show you what to
    prevent,

Simply ask people you trust for their help and what they believe,
And a much truer picture of yourself you are sure to achieve,

Then go to work on yourself occasionally asking those friends
    for feedback,
And use their objective point of view to keep you on an ever
    improving track.

INSPIRATION_____

There are times when we've seen others perform to an outstanding
    extreme,
They show us what's possible if we'll simply follow our dream,

Like breaking the four minute mile and feats similar in scope,
They make us believe in possibilities, they give us some hope,

And on many of these occasions tears are shed by those looking on,
For it makes us realize there's more than we imagined to the human
    phenomenon,

Perhaps we also saw what we could have been or could still be,
If we just followed our heart's desire and let our spirits free,

Yes we were inspired because we realized that they're only
    human too,
And we could also achieve greatness if we'd simply follow our
    dream through,

Either way, their accomplishment will bring a brighter day
    than before,
Because they've shown us that human beings possess even more,

And if what they did is possible, what else could we dare,
If we pushed for our best without giving fear a care,

Inspiration is great because it rekindles our grand vision,
It reminds us it's never too late for a life-changing decision,

So remember movies, memories, and events which inspired you
    in some way,
Then keep constant reminders of them around you as you go
    through your day,

You'll find the inspiration keeps you focused in the proper direction,
And you'll notice your life's purpose and motivation will experience
    a great resurrection.

THE DEATHBED TEST_____

Each of us moves through life thinking it will last forever,
The time of our death seems no closer than never,

We don't have enough time to do what must be done,
Yet there's always plenty of time to do things that are fun,

After work comes and we're simply too tired,
Our truly important projects are the first to get fired,

After all it's difficult to simply get through our day,
Focusing on the small picture becomes clearly our way,

For what's important to us can wait, there's always more time,
Then twenty years pass and we find our life has died on the vine,

We must accept our mortality and put ourselves at the end,
Or we'll find our bad tendencies quite unwilling to bend,

Place yourself on your deathbed and take a look behind,
Then what's really important you're likely to find,

If your life continues as is, you'll see what is lost,
You'll catch your bad habits and their ultimate cost,

Change your ways until your vision brings much peace of mind,
And your energy and enthusiasm you'll once again find,

The impulse to work on unimportant tasks will suddenly reverse,
When you see the big picture and your special role in the universe.

Is That All There Is _____

Many times we get caught up chasing what we think will make us
    pleased,
Then we finally get that item only to find our longing has not eased,

We thought we'd be so much more excited to find ourselves in
    this place,
Then we arrive at our destination to find that's not the case,

So we continue along the same path trying for bigger and better still,
Then we achieve those lofty goals, yet that desire we can't fulfill,

"Is That All There Is?", we'll continue to ask if we use goals in
    this fashion,
The only way to avoid this is to work inside ourselves with passion,

For items in the outside world cannot correct what's wrong
    deep inside,
And no amount of external possessions will help those issues hide,

We must look in the mirror and decide the person we'd really
    like to be,
We'll only be truly happy when we're content with the person
    known as me,

Then we can go after outside goods to enhance the life we already
    enjoy,
Instead of looking for happiness in an outside material toy,

For the purpose of a goal, dream, or desire is not to mark a certain
    conclusion,
To believe that any of the above will consummate our happiness is
    simply an illusion,

Realize each goal is a part of the process and there's life after each
    win or defeat,
And you'll see life as a journey and won't look to one event to make
    your life complete.

IT'S A CHILD'S WORLD ⎯⎯⎯⎯⎯⎯

I see children play and they seem so carefree,
They don't see black and white or difference; they get along
    willingly,

They relate so well even to those they've just met,
Their minds are free of prejudice, bias, and all other judgment,

Their dreams are so big, whatever they wish for is possible,
Anything their imagination can come up with is much more
    than probable,

They seem to fear nothing and charge ahead at full speed,
If there's something in their way they refuse to let it impede,

They work well together, not many words need to be said,
It seems their endless supply of energy never needs to be fed,

They're not afraid to be different or stand out in a crowd,
They don't temper their actions; they speak their minds aloud,

They have grandiose dreams of what they'll be in the future,
They're convinced they can be anything, such big hopes they
    nurture,

 Yes, it's a Child's World in which possibilities are endless,
Against their positive outlook, negatives are defenseless.

AGAINST ALL ODDS _____

One of the most important parts of life is to constantly grow,
We all possess much more than we'll probably ever know,

Yet so few of us push and challenge ourselves to be more,
At the first sign of difficulty we walk out the door,

The odds may seem high but with enough persistence we can prevail,
Even though the most important part isn't even if we win or we fail,

The person we'll become in the process is the most critical part,
The journey will help to develop our mind and our heart,

For there is much more inside than we'll ever use,
How high and far we want to go is up to us to choose,

The greater the obstacle, the greater conquering it will feel,
Becoming more of a person is the best part of the deal,

So don't let things seem impossible, believe in who you are,
Pursue anything you dream of, reach your unreachable star,

And even if the odds seem against you, don't ever give in,
Push ahead with determination, be driven to win,

The odds will turn in your favor, once you've won in your mind,
Then resources you didn't know you possessed will now be easy
    to find,

Forget about the odds and focus on the person you'll be when
    the journey is done,
Or you'll always look back on your life and wonder what you
    could have become.

LAUGHTER _____

Laughter is quite wonderful, it's the music of the soul,
Most hope that at their own expense, its likeness doesn't toll,

It's good to be able to laugh at ourselves but never at another,
As far a cure for stress and anxiety, laughter's better than any other,

It's also good to laugh with others, at a good story or joke,
Just make sure someone's misfortune isn't the subject at which
    you poke,

Doctors tell us it's important to have a good laugh everyday,
Laughter fights illness and has other health benefits they say,

It sets off chemical changes in our bodies, the results of which
    are good,
It takes our focus off of adversity and helps us see the things we
    should,

Laughter helps to put things in perspective, for what they really
    should be,
We realize something's not that big a deal, the bigger picture we see,

Things that now seem major, we'll laugh about years down the road,
Why not find what's funny today and lighten your current load,

So decide what's really important and take seriously that which is
    essential,
And try to find the funny side and laugh at that which is
    inconsequential.

Learn from Others' Mistakes _____

As we go through this life we can learn on our own,
Or, we can choose to learn from what others have sown,

Those that have gone before us have made every mistake,
They've realized each miscue in all activities in which we partake,

Why should we repeat errors that have been made in the past,
If we avoid them, we'll find our progress increases quite fast,

We'll cut down on time necessary to achieve our goal,
Problems and huddles will take much less of a toll,

Yes others have paved the road, the way down it they've shown,
Let's follow their map instead of making our own,

We can get so much farther if we'll learn from others before,
We can start from where they left off and travel some more,

Our most valuable resource is time and mistakes take it away,
The more we avoid, the more time we'll create in the day,

So learn from others' mistakes and also from what they did right,
And your life will have far fewer hurdles and be a less bumpy flight.

STOP AND SMELL THE ROSES ―――――

As we walk on this planet and carry on with our day,
There are many things around us to which no attention we pay,

They're small things that I assume are easy to miss,
So we don't even see them in our unconscious bliss,

Our days are pretty much the same since we're creatures of routine,
So as a result many things go sight unseen,

Yet many of these small wonders are what life's all about,
We take them for granted day in and day out,

We should appreciate life and what it has to give,
We dwell in a world in which many miracles live,

There are the animals around us, the flowers and trees,
The beautiful sunsets, the birds, and the bees,

There are the people we assume will be there for all time,
There's our health, our freedom, and also our good mind,

Take time to appreciate these gifts and how lucky you are,
Notice those things that we leave mentally quite afar,

Look at life for a day as if tomorrow you'll be gone,
Then many things you haven't noticed will instantly dawn,

Smell a flower, take a walk, stop and look around you,
You'll suddenly appreciate life more and be happier too.

LOVE YOURSELF BEFORE ANOTHER___

There's a question that's crossed my mind at least a time or two,
Can someone not love them self yet love another through and
    through,

It seems the greatest love is that which for ourselves we hold in
    store,
If one does not know this love, would they know another knocking
    at their door,

Like material possessions, those of the soul must be owned before
    given away,
It seems those without self love tend to hold others at bay,

If when someone thinks of themselves they have no love or respect,
What kind of a reception can anyone else possibly expect,

For if they feel they are not worthy and someone were to love and
    respect them,
From these unfamiliar feelings many misunderstandings would
    surely stem,

Our outward world is but a mirror of how we feel inside,
Unless you settle things within yourself you're in for a difficult ride,

So if you can't find what you're looking for, turn your focus within,
Once you find truth and understanding inside, with your new
    attitude you'll win,

Remember, you don't need to hope for love, create it inside then
    give it out,
Whatever you give will return tenfold to you, it will come back
    without a doubt.

MAKE LIFE A STUDY_____

As life goes by most hope to pick up what they need to survive,
Yet osmosis alone will rarely get us what we need to thrive,

If we're to become fluent in a subject we must dissect it well,
Others who have studied it before us, its story they tell,

We can find a wealth of knowledge in books, tapes and the like,
They sit on shelves waiting for our intelligence to strike,

There are answers on raising happy families, money, and investing,
If we'd just take the time to do some information digesting,

People would like to know more, however, they find themselves
too busy,
With no experience they wonder why the decisions make them
dizzy,

They figure they'll just wing it, surely everything will be okay,
Or there'll be time tomorrow, they'll save it for another day,

So they leave the most important items in their life open to chance,
While all the answers are so close, all about them they dance,

It's only years down the road they realize they could have done
more,
They look at life's most important issues and see their education
is poor,

We don't need to reinvent the wheel, or, for that matter sliced
bread,
We do MUCH better in subjects in which we're well-read,

So study a subject vigorously if its content you wish to rule,
Or you're likely to find your experience with that subject quite
cruel.

MASTERY _____

In order to master a subject you must study it every day,
Total immersion and keeping up-to-date is the only way,

In this fast-paced world nearly all industries change fast,
In some, taking a few months off is enough to be left in the past,

Yet while you keep up, you must remember the fundamentals,
They will build your foundation and take care of the incidentals,

Once you've mastered the basics you must still practice them much,
Or when you go to use them down the road they'll be out of touch,

And when you've achieved the above, improve on what has been
       done,
Breaking new ground by shattering old limitations is half of the fun,

For each area of specialty has room to progress,
In fact if it doesn't, eventually it will completely regress,

Master your subject by spending at least an hour a day in review,
Find as many books and tapes as you can possibly preview,

Also talk to as many people as you can that are involved in the trade,
Seek the most prominent and successful people that the industry's
       made,

Learn to be fascinated with the subject and have an absolute need to
       be the best,
And all the pieces will fall into place as forces of nature take care of
       the rest.

MID—LIFE CRISIS _____

As we start out our lives, we have many grandiose dreams and
   visions,
As children our hopes are many and our wants have no limiting
   provisions,

Then as the years start to pass, we get caught up living day-to-day,
The world beats us up a bit and we begin to become "Realistic"
   along the way,

We put those "Big Dreams" on hold for now, we'll achieve them
   down the road,
After all we've got many years to get after them, presently they're
   too heavy a load,

Then as more time passes we get in the habit of putting them
   further back,
Until one day we wake up only to find we've fallen way off track,

We remember our dreams of the past and our desires deep within,
Yet now there's so much more to do and much less time to do it in,

We start to panic and do strange things, afraid our chance has past,
We start to take drastic measures fearful that in stone our future's
   cast,

We realize our life is half over and our ultimate project has not
   yet begun,
We discover we've wasted our life on urgent unimportant tasks
   and having too much fun,

So now we must do something crazy to make us think we have
   more time,
We try things to make us look years younger and convince ourselves
   all is fine,

Yet that approach is not realistic, it's important to take a different
    view,
We must start to ask ourselves what we want and think the answers
    through,

The most critical thing to remember is not to panic at this fateful
    hour,
Realize you have some time and your destination is still under your
    own power,

The next step is to write down some goals, to give you some
    direction,
You don't have to be perfect, you can always make a course
    correction,

Make them easy but challenging and have the outcomes clear,
Be excited that a more meaningful future is getting increasingly near,

So start today by remembering what's important and your desires
    deep inside,
Be determined to make a difference and to enjoy life's exciting ride.

REAP WHAT YOU SOW_____

When someone puts forward a half-hearted attempt at a mission,
I'm amazed when they don't understand the resulting poor vision,

The projects in which we're involved will reflect our attempt,
They'll show whether we face a task with respect or contempt,

Yes, we tend to reap what we sow in each and every action,
With a strong effort, usually, we'll succeed to our satisfaction,

People's living areas tend to reflect what goes on in their mind,
Whether cleanliness, or, cluttered that's what you'll surely find,

If we're careless and messy, that will tend to show,
If mindful and caring, our surroundings will let others know,

If confused over something and pulled in two directions,
The work we produce will typically be riddled with corrections,

Difficulty with one area of life many times carries to others,
Our creative insight and ability to problem solve it often smothers,

Understand that the labor we put in will reflect our final reward,
It'll show whether the project inspired us or left us quite bored,

So try to put your heart and soul into each task in which you
    partake,
The ultimate result will reflect upon you, your reputation's at stake.

NEGATIVE EMOTIONS _____

They steal our life blood, our greatest hopes and dreams,
They kill our relationships and from them bitterness streams,

They sap our strength, destroy our hope and inside create deadly
    potions,
They serve no purpose and clutter our life, they're negative
emotions,

We know the damage they can do, yet in them we partake,
We see the misery and the destructive lives they can make,

We can decide to let them go and live more happy than gray,
Good feelings and emotions can turn around the most miserable day,

The best way to fight negative emotions is to get beneficial ones in
    our head,
Do this by focusing on positive things you've heard, seen or perhaps
    even read,

Another good idea is to keep our goals with us to keep us on track,
When we see the big picture, negatives tend to roll off our back,

Then there's a simple choice to look for the good in each situation,
You'll find it's not that difficult if you use a little creation,

Just keep in mind negative feelings take you in the wrong direction,
If you're determined not to be beaten, you'll make the necessary
    correction,

Yes, life is a game in which negative emotions are a block,
The more you indulge in them, the more time they'll steal from
    your clock,

Take them as a challenge and realize you have a choice in how
    you feel,
The earlier you learn to beat them, the better you'll deal,

So use negative emotions either to temporarily inspire you or,
    get rid of them all together,
Once you get in the habit you'll change your life faster than ever.

NEW YEAR'S RESOLUTIONS _____

Around the same time each year we make the same move,
And hope that somehow this time, we'll stay in the groove,

We don't change our approach, yet hope this year will be unique,
We expect this New Year's Eve to suddenly have some extra
  mystique,

Though New Year's Resolutions have failed in the past in spite of
  our best,
For some reason we think this New Year will be different from
  the rest,

We start with the best of intentions and plenty of drive,
Yet we become discouraged when success doesn't quickly arrive,

Yes, the newness of the New Year persists to carry us for a bit,
But it's eventually no match for our new behavior's uncomfortable
  fit,

A New Year doesn't have enough intensity to make us transform,
Its psychological power isn't white hot, it's maybe lukewarm,

You must find much stronger motivation to do what you must do,
Only compelling emotional reasons will carry you through,

Begin by not waiting until the New Year, start toward your goals
  today,
And try something different with good reasons to make your new
  habits stay,

Then use the New Year to celebrate the new you that's been
  discovered,
And the real secrets of lasting change you've finally uncovered.

ONE DAY AT A TIME _____

Sometimes we focus on the big picture and the view is just too
  much,
We are frozen by fear, it's overwhelming, when we look at it as
  such,

We must take things in smaller chunks so the task does not defeat
  us,
If we see too much to be done, just the thought of the project will
  beat us,

Realize that every ten thousand mile journey starts with a single
  pace,
If we take things in smaller pieces, we've got a better chance of
  finishing the race,

If we break a huge project into little goals, we'll make it slow but
  sure,
Doing small amounts each day, instead of all at once, we'll actually
  accomplish more,

If we make our goals too large, we'll doubt our ability to get it
  completed,
We may start the project but soon we're likely to find we're
  mentally defeated,

The trick is to be somewhere in the middle, challenging yet
  believable,
The only way we'll see it through is if it excites us and we
  KNOW it's achievable,

We must focus on the present and what we have to do on that
  given day,
If day-to-day we meet our goals, then on our path we'll stay,

Even if we have a bad day or two, once they're over let them rest,

Focus only on TODAY, the present, give THIS day your best,

So instead of always looking at the huge picture, take one day at
    a time,
If each day you do what needs to be done, your future will be fine.

Our Own Little World_____

I had a strange dream of a world in which everyone was just like me,
Watching others gave me an objective view, my qualities and
   attributes were easy to see,

This world had things missing which were no longer important
   or in need,
However, it also lacked some variety and diversity it needed
   more indeed,

Yet this dream raised an interesting question that had not crossed
   my mind before,
What if everyone in the world were just like me, would our
   planet be less or more?

This question helped me take inventory of my actions, it helped me
   see the light,
With a worldly vision I saw long term effects and gained completely
   new insight,

If everyone were doing the same as me, the results would show
   much faster,
I started to realize though some actions seemed small, they were
   leading to disaster,

However, I also saw some positives which needed more direction
   and more vision,
These were ways I could make the world better, starting with a
   simple decision,

I came to the realization that my world would be a pretty good
   place,
What if everyone were just like me, it's a question all of us should
   face,

That's one way to find out how we feel about ourselves deep

down inside,
When we see things on a larger scale, they're more difficult to hide,

So ask yourself the question and see if you can answer true,
Then go to work on yourself and change till you like your world
    through and through.

PAYING THE PRICE _____

There is simply no shortcut to success, that much is true,
And it will stay true no matter how much you otherwise construe,

In order to make your own way there's a price you must pay,
Someone else cannot pave your road, or clear your way,

For success must be something inside, that you yourself possess,
And when you're standing all alone, that you're ready to address,

You must have your own experience on which to fall back,
When defeat and despair are threatening to throw you off track,

It's important to have many encounters as opposed to a few,
The more background you have, the more likely you'll get through,

And it's certain that the more you've prepared the luckier you'll be,
The smarter and harder you work, the brighter future you'll see,

So decide what you're after and the price to be paid,
Then make sure a plan for its achievement has been laid,

You must expend fully for what you desire, there's no other way out,
Simply deciding what you want, then paying the price is what life's
    all about.

PERSPECTIVE _____

Most of the time we rush through our day without even a second
     thought,
Fully 99 percent of us don't realize how lucky we got,

Every once in awhile we should stop and realize how gifted we are,
Most of us have a pretty good life, most of us fell under a lucky star,

When you look at the death and disease and problems that abound,
In our own lives, I think most of us realize few problems are found,

Oh sure we've all experienced a tragedy or, difficulty from time to
     time,
And probably more than 90 percent of our lives go along just fine,

Everything is relative though, we compare to what we know,
For some simply sitting in traffic seems a difficult blow,

Yet there are worse things in life if we really do ponder,
And no matter how bad it seems, it could be worse over yonder,

Yes, we appreciate what is no longer and absence makes the heart
     fond,
Why not be thankful for what we have right now and that special
     bond,

Perspective is different depending upon where you choose to stand,
It will affect the outcome of your life and were you eventually land,

So try to see the good in your life and decide to expect only the
     best,
If you can do that each and every day, you'll triumph in any life test.

MORE PERSPECTIVE _____

I led them to water, yet they returned looking for drink,
I tried to direct them, but from my viewpoint, they were unable
    to think,

In pleading with them, I talked till I was blue in the face,
Yet they must see on their own, they must make their own case,

People will see what they want to see, regardless of truth,
It can make us act strangely, many times without couth,

We must find our own way through this world, each and everyone,
When it comes to life and living, personal experience is second to
    none,

So the next time you're adamant another is making a mistake,
And you carry the worry of another's actions in which they partake,

Remember, experiences shape our viewpoints and make that vision
    our own,
We must let others make their own destiny and reap what they've
    sown.

Recording Your Life_____

Some among us record our lives in a journal or book,
It seems to get feelings out and give a more objective look,

It can also help us in similar situations down the road,
To see what worked and what didn't as we handled the load,

It may also help us remember an idea we thought up a while back,
Or give us some perspective to keep us on track,

A journal can be a teaching tool to help those that come after,
It may help in future successes or in avoiding disaster,

In any case, it's good to have an account of our existence in this
    place,
If for nothing else, it can help relatives with the roots that they
    trace,

A journal is a record that will be here after we pass on,
A part of ourselves to remind others we're not really gone,

For our wisdom and experience is there for others to live,
Then although we're gone we're still able to give,

So if your life is worth living, make sure you record it each day,
And more in touch with your world and living you're likely to stay.

Sportsmanship_____

There are many events in our lives in which we'll win or lose,
How we react to both of those outcomes is up to us to choose,

The final result is not always the most important part,
It's how we decide to view it in our head and our heart,

Some walk around after a win and think they must brag,
For others around, that's really a drag,

You've heard of sore losers, yet there are sore winners too,
No one likes either, that much is true,

We'll probably win a time or two so how we handle it is key,
You'll deal with it most courteously if the other person's side you
    see,

It comes back to how we treat others and the golden rule,
Be kind and understanding, don't ever be cruel,

For you'll surely be defeated, just as at other times you've won,
Then if the winner boasts and gloats, you'll see it's no fun,

Whether winning or losing, try to view your opponent the same,
Your attitude during and after the match is the most crucial part
    of the game.

ROLL WITH THE PUNCHES _____

In our lives we'll run into situations we don't expect,
How we handle those events is an important aspect,

When things get crazy it's easy to make them seem great,
Keeping perspective at these times is a critical trait,

We must keep our heads and try to stay cool,
Calmness is a very important tool,

For when we blow things out of proportion we usually don't
  act right,
We end up taking dangerous measures or even causing a fight,

The best thing to do is to stop and consider the situation,
There's usually an amiable way out if we use a little creation,

We should always be ready for something unexpected to occur,
If we're prepared, any problem's sure to cause less of a stir,

For one of the greatest qualities is the ability to adapt,
If we're ready for anything, then to major mistakes we're less apt,

So learn to roll with the punches by expecting that which you
  could not foresee,
You'll find life a much smoother ride and with less catastrophes
  it will be.

Say What?_____

It's interesting how much of a role language plays in our sphere,
Just by saying a few words either intelligent, or not, we appear,

The ability to express ourselves is obviously important,
Yet it's amazing how many people's grasp of their language is
    absolutely abhorrent,

Those with good language skills seem to travel quite far,
While those with poor talent have much difficulty just staying par,

We tend to pick up speech habits from parents and those with
    whom we live,
Unfortunately, if they have bad habits, it's those which they'll
    tend to give,

We can work to improve our grammar, though few rarely do,
Usually the ones enhancing their speech are those that least need to,

Most of us simply stop learning by the time school is out,
At that point we usually have only a vague idea of what our
    language is about,

Others will judge you by your vocabulary, both of pen and of voice,
How others ultimately see you is completely your choice,

By words you can move mountains and draw others to your side,
Or you can push people away and through indifference, divide,

So realize the better your language skills the more pleasure you'll
    discover,
The worse your skills, the more problems you're likely to uncover,

So if your speech is already outstanding, build it in addition,
If it's fair or poor, study and work until it's in excellent condition.

SAY WHAT YOU MEAN_____

As I looked at our language and the spoken word,
I began to dig deeper and soon certain things occurred,

One is that words are important, but only part of the meaning,
The tone of voice we use is also relevant, be it kind or demeaning,

The gestures we make are also important,
You can say something nice yet your body language is abhorrent,

Facial expressions and where we look also play a key role,
If they're out of line we can look like we're selling our soul,

The last part of a sentence holds importance and how it should end,
An up note or down note can be the difference in the message we
    send,

Even the speed of our words can affect what we say,
It can add confusion to words we speak everyday,

In addition to all of the above, there's also voice inflection,
It can give the meaning of words quite a different reflection,

So make sure what and how you say something are the right fit,
Because ultimately both will determine how your words sit.

SETTLING FOR LESS _____

It's funny how as life goes on, we start to settle for what's there,
It seems as if after a while, it becomes too much work to care,

We convince ourselves it's good enough, it's all we can expect,
We live half a life as a result, our frail egos we protect,

We let our fears get in the way and keep us from first prize,
It eventually becomes a domino effect and our confidence slowly
    dies,

Things we want may not come easy, that's the way this world is
    made,
Many of us give up and give in, our hopes and dreams we trade,

We tell ourselves again and again, we're not worthy of the top
    award,
Then we wake each day to find it's the bottom we're moving toward,

We stop fighting for what we aspire to and settle for less than the
    best,
Anything worth it is difficult work, we can't have it without a test,

We must decide we're fed up with less and raise our standards high,
This is the first step that will turn our focus to the sky,

We must decide it's a worthy cause, the pain will be worth the gain,
Or we'll find ourselves on the sidelines, from anything meaningful
    we'll abstain,

There's only one way to move in this world which will give you any
    pride,
It's moving up and onward and being part of a life changing ride,

For once we give up and settle, our life is on the downward slope,
Our world will become virtually meaningless once we've learned to
    give up hope,

So find some fight deep inside and make your dreams come true,
The extra juice you get from your experiences will carry your spirit
through,

And if you're at the end of your rope, tie a knot and hang on,
If you continue to persist long enough, you'll reach the coming
dawn.

STUPID IS AS STUPID DOES_____

Our intelligence does not always show in each and every action,
Many times we do things much to our own dissatisfaction,

For we can be the smartest person in the universe,
Yet our conduct may indicate the exact reverse,

Simply having the brains is not the entire story,
Our actions can still lead either to defeat or to glory,

You can be intelligent but act stupid if you don't think things
    through,
And at the same time, the opposite also rings true,

Your Intelligence Quotient can only reveal your potential,
Whether you act with smarts is the only fact that's consequential,

For if you act in a way that is stupid, then stupid you are,
If you act in a way that is outstanding, then you're a star,

We've all seen people with everything, yet they throw it away,
And people with nothing that rise to conquer the day,

The difference is what they decide to do with what they possess,
The choice is up to us whether we'll grow or regress,

And though it's true we all have intelligence to a different degree,
Regardless of this fact, there's only one truth that will set you free,

By not challenging yourself and growing, any potential you have
    dies,
No matter what your level of intelligence, doing your best makes
    you wise.

SURVIVOR _____

The game of life starts immediately upon our planetary arrival,
Whether or not we realize it, we're constantly in a challenge for
    survival,

It starts with just being conceived and the odds which we face,
And continues through gestation and our birth to this place,

Then we encounter more hurdles when as children we sprout,
And walk around with unknown dangers continually about,

We try our best in sports, school, and similar endeavors,
To excel at activities that adults and our peers use as measures,

And as we get older, we constantly compare ourselves to others,
It makes no difference even if they're sisters or brothers,

Though this isn't bad if it inspires us to constantly evolve,
As long as around bad intentions it doesn't revolve,

Yes simply living on the planet for a number of years is no easy feat,
With all the things that could go wrong, it's admirable not to fall to
    defeat,

All of us are survivors in this big world where we dwell,
One in which what tomorrow will bring is sometimes difficult
    to tell,

So appreciate life and what it took to come this far,
And cherish all you've become and the survivor you are.

THE BEST YOU CAN DO IS
THE BEST YOU CAN DO———————

There are times when we'll give our best effort yet we'll still fail,
How we handle those defeats is an important detail,

At these times it's common for us to take things a bit tough,
It's usually ourselves who, on us, can be the most rough,

It's not easy to keep things in perspective at times such as this,
We seem to only be able to focus on that which is amiss,

It's more difficult if we think there was more we could have done,
Though it's not easy even if we've covered everything under the sun,

The thing to remember is that you can only do so much,
There comes a point when it's simply out of your touch,

We could all stand on our heads twenty-four hours a day,
But is the reward ultimately worth the price we would pay,

The best rule is to make sure you've done all you can reasonably do,
Then once your part is over, let the situation carry on through,

The question may come up as to where that final line should be,
Inside you know what's reasonable, your gut feelings will help you
    see,

Just do the best you can do, then realize it's out of your hands,
You can't always completely control where the ball lands,

Give it all you've got and when you've done your part rest,
For the most that you can ever do is your absolute best.

THE IMPORTANCE OF BEING A SELF—STARTER _____

You see it in the greatest amongst us, in those that set the trend,
It's a fire burning deep inside that carries them to the end,

In those who don't do much with their lives this fire can't be found,
They look for others to spur them on and never get off the ground,

The winner realizes no one else can run their life, or tell them
    what to do,
They have to find their own purpose and reasons to act and
    see things through,

It's the champions who look to themselves for what they need to
    live,
They're constantly searching to improve and for more areas to give,

They feed their minds, they feed their bodies, they feed their souls
    with good,
They realize that true fulfillment comes from faith and brotherhood,

They don't look outside themselves to justify their actions,
They listen to the voice inside to guide their interactions,

They know their destiny is up to them, they're in complete control,
Their life is not determined by fate, the stars or cards of tarot,

They are clear on what they want from life, their highest ideals
    they know,
That is what wakes them early and keeps them on the go,

So find a cause, if you don't have one already, for which you'll give
    your all,
When you'll do something regardless of money or fame, you have
    truly found your call.

THE POWER WITHIN_____

Successful people are successful well before they do anything great,
Success isn't something on the outside, it's actually an internal trait,

Before you reach the mountain top, the attainment is already within,
It's pent up potential waiting for the journey to begin,

Everything you need to be outstanding is already inside,
Your life can either be boring or a most exciting ride,

For just because it's there doesn't mean it will be used well,
That's an answer to a question that only time can tell,

Yet the power is there if you'll put yourself to the test,
The ability to outdo prior achievements and break the world's best,

Yes, if you only decide, you can be number one,
And your life can be one full of adventure and fun,

For the power within sets no limits at all,
It simply sits and waits for you to answer the call,

You can live an unoriginal life or one quite unique,
The answers are there, they hold no real mystique,

You have the ability to learn, plan and do all that's required,
To achieve anything that, past or present, you may have desired,

So don't be afraid to fail, for inside yourself victory you already
    hold,
Go out and write the most amazing story of human achievement
    that's ever been told.

THE PERSON IN THE MIRROR⎯⎯⎯⎯

When the world seems difficult and things aren't coming up right,
Begin by looking at yourself before you go starting a fight,

Many times there are attitudes and receptions that follow us around,
We wonder what's wrong with everyone else when within us the
    answer is found,

If you don't like the demeanor of others and they seem to have a
    bad attitude,
Look inside yourself to see if an answer can be construed,

For it's certain that for each action there's an equal and
    opposite reaction,
This is true of human relations in every single social transaction,

You'll find one person can go somewhere and people are great,
Then another goes to find people there possess a nasty trait,

Maybe it's the individual person and how they treat others,
With a negative approach, a warm welcome it smothers,

Ask what it is inside of you that makes others react a certain way,
It's probably one simple behavior that causes others to move away
    or stay,

And on a smaller scale, when out of communication with one
    other being,
Try to understand their position and the view from which they
    are seeing,

For people's reactions to us are like a mirror reflecting back what
    we show,
As with anything in life those reactions reap what we sow,

So if you want all the mysteries of how the planet welcomes you
    unfurled,
Start by looking in the mirror to find what's right and wrong with
    the world.

THE RESPONSIBILITY OF IRRESPONSIBILITY_____

I heard the statistics, they were really quite alarming,
Yet my own situation left anything I could say less than disarming,

As others congratulate a child for giving birth to the same,
I wonder what's happen to our perspective, in fact our good name,

We praise those so different, those willing to bend and break the
rules most cruelly,
The examples they've set, coupled with our selfishness, have made
things quite unruly,

We want to blame others, anyone but ourselves for each callus
mistake,
We fail to take responsibility and credit for the actions in which
we partake,

Oh it's not the fault of him or her it's the system or institution,
Teaching others not to take responsibility will bring our
nonexistence to fruition,

Consider the source and both sides before rushing to judgment,
We may see things much more clearly if we'll let our intelligence
ferment,

The long-term cost of irresponsible behavior weighs heavy on
ourselves and others,
It's tearing us down as a whole, we're in this together, we're all
sisters and brothers,

There is no easy way out, sometimes it's difficult to do what
we know is right,
Yet it makes us better people, we gain strength and character
through the fight,

Every great society has fallen unable to stand the time test,

It's not too late, we can dig deep and bring out our best,

We must do what we can in our own little corner of the universe,
Each of us can make a difference, it's the only way to make our
situation reverse,

So do what you can and make a stand for a worthy cause of your
choice,
Take responsibility, do what you can, and when in doubt, listen to
that little voice.

RESPONSIBILITY————————————————

More and more these days when someone's actions lead to trouble,
They are very unwilling to take blame and burst their own bubble,

They could be seen by many and even caught in the act,
Yet no matter how much evidence, it's interesting to see them react,

They point the finger at others and any outside event,
They'll insist it was impossible for them to prevent,

They'll call it a disease or something wrong with their past,
They swear whatever it is, the effects will not last,

If you're looking for blame for where you are and what you do,
Look in the mirror and the culprit will be staring back at you,

We are most happy when our lives are under our control,
When making decisions in our world we must be in the starring
    role,

The only way to be in control is to take responsibility for all that
    you are,
When you realize your life is up to you, you'll travel quite far,

So understand you're the star, you can get the job done,
By taking responsibility you'll find your self-esteem you have won,

Take control of your life by taking responsibility and facing your
    fears,
Or you'll find your world in turmoil, full of heartache and tears.

THE TRUTH _____

People say to believe half of what you see and none of what you
    hear,
However, I believe the writing's on the wall, it's the message we fear,

Though the truth, deep down inside, we're really quite certain,
It's the fear of the unknown that stops us from drawing the final
    curtain,

When in doubt, it's best to trust the truth in your gut,
Its vision is crystal clear even with eyes completely shut,

For the eventual fate you will surely someday know,
Sooner or later, the decisions up to you, you're running the show,

Still the devil we know must be better than the one down the road,
That's the belief that will force you to continue to carry that load,

The truth your heart knows is not going away,
It's the fear of the short term pain that makes us unwilling to sway,

So we avoid the truth to make the present seem fine,
Thus our future is sacrificed, that's the bottom line,

So summon your courage and act on what you KNOW to be true,
Or you'll continue to carry needless pain and sorrow your whole
    life through.

CHOICE _____

Sometimes we have many options, other times only a few,
You're not in too bad shape if you have more than two,

It's important to realize that we always have some control,
Even if we're in jail with no possible chance of parole,

In the worst possible cases we can still manage our mind,
There are remedies and solutions if we'll only seek and find,

Even prisoners of war can decide what to take from their ordeal,
They can determine how their captors can and can't make them feel,

This may sound a little extreme and difficult to believe true,
Yet you'll see it's correct if you study the facts through,

Choice leads to control, which is what our lives are based upon,
The more control we have, the less we feel like a pawn,

For when we're in charge of our destiny all else falls into place,
And we believe we belong to this world and have our own special
    space,

So when the night seems the darkest, realize you still have some
    power,
And there's always a choice, even in your most desperate hour,

The situation may seem futile yet you always have a voice,
Your outlook, your attitude, and your demeanor are always your
    choice.

Things We Take for Granted ⎯⎯⎯⎯

It's funny the things we don't appreciate as we walk through our day,
We have been given many great gifts for which we'd happily pay,

The things we take for granted are abundant, they're everywhere,
We'd surely miss them if all of a sudden they were no longer there,

Most of us get up everyday and go about life without a hitch,
We don't realize there are many areas in which we are truly rich,

Most of us have the ability to see, hear, and talk,
If we lost those abilities, our life would be a much different walk,

You see Helen Keller, missing the two most important tools of
    perception,
Yet she became more than most able-bodied people, she made her
    life an exception,

For even if we lose one of our abilities and we feel a little less free,
There are still plenty of other gifts we have, if we'll take the time
    to see,

We're independent and can make decisions on our own,
We decide what we want to reap and what we want sown,

We can move freely through our world, till the dusk from the dawn,
We really won't realize how lucky we are until one of our abilities
    is gone,

That's okay, after all, to think about those things would surely take
    time,
However, next time you're depressed, just a few of these things can
    make you feel fine,

Realize what you have going for you, that some others no longer
    possess,
Then perhaps on your small problems, you'll no longer obsess,

Yes, the ability to hear, see, walk, and talk are great,
When it comes to living, good health is a most important trait,

So thank God for what you haven't lost and for what you still retain,
Live with gratitude and from most negatives your life will refrain.

TIME OUT_____

You should take some time each day to figure things out,
Fifteen minutes or so to think of what life's all about,

The world as a whole and your place in it,
Your relationship with yourself and where you sit,

A time in quiet when you focus inside,
One in which you put all other matters aside,

Somewhere alone with nobody but you,
Where you think your thoughts completely through,

Yes, getting in touch with feelings deep down in the heart,
Is the beginning of self-discovery and the most important part,

Some sort of meditation should be a part of each day,
For mental fitness has an important role to play,

Accept yourself, your feelings and all you've become,
Appreciate what you've been through and where you've come from,

Take this time to think about what you want to be,
Get a clear vision of the final outcome you'd like to see,

Let negatives and bad feelings leave you and keep all the rest,
Prepare for anything, yet, expect only the best.

TO ERR IS HUMAN _____

As human beings we'll occasionally make a mistake,
Yet the more we dwell on past ones the more we'll make,

To be perfect all the time isn't part of the plan,
All we can simply do is the best that we can,

The trick is to realize this and use it the right way,
We must hold a high standard yet not let it ruin our day,

For on the one hand we can take a mistake way too hard,
On the other, we can take it too easily and growth we retard,

We must look at the situation and try to erase its cause,
This takes some thorough study, it takes some pause,

Just realize a life lived fully will have plenty of errors,
And we must control them so they don't turn into terrors,

For the fear will stop us before we ever begin,
Then we'll never be in a position in which we can win,

Successful people make the most mistakes and understand more
        from each one,
If you learn from lots of mistakes you'll experience success by the
        ton,

So remember, mistakes make you more intelligent and more able to
        discern,
They are part of being human and our greatest opportunity to learn.

To Thine Own Voice Be True_____

Many of us live our lives day-to-day, running in the gerbil wheel,
We lose focus on the big picture and our life loses its zeal,

We also face many difficult decisions and endless tough choices,
When things are the most confusing, we hear the most opinions
and voices,

Yet there is a source that cuts through the turmoil, it always rings
true,
It comes from a spot in the back of our minds, it always knows
what to do,

Some feel the voice is gone after years of trying to fit in, afraid
to stand out,
It seems as if the voice has quieted, or, disappeared, drowned in
self-doubt,

Yet the wisdom is still there, waiting for us to wake up and take
charge,
It's ready to help us to achieve anything, it wants us to live large,

So if you already listen to that voice, continue to respect it and
follow its scheme,
And if you don't, start to listen now and chase your every dream.

Belief _____

I've heard it said that seeing is believing, but I think the opposite
  is so,
In order to see you must first believe, its presence you must know,

If you believe with all your being that a certain fact is true,
You'll operate as if it's so, it will be reality for you,

If you believe you can or you believe you can't, you're right more
  often than not,
Your belief of what's inside of you will determine how much
  you've got,

Your world reflects your beliefs and what you feel deep down,
They determine whether you face challenges with a smile or frown,

Your beliefs dictate what you'll do, what you'll think and what
  you'll say,
Learn to change those that limit you or a terrible price you'll pay,

All things you desire are possible once you develop the belief,
Empowering growth is feasible and will save you from much grief,

So if you're not happy with a part of your life, change your reality
  perception,
It's undoubtedly your truths in that area which hold you back
  without exception,

If you want to possess certain beliefs and traits, act as if you
  already do,
Many times simply pretending like this is enough to carry you
  through,

For you can be and do anything if you believe it deep down in your
  soul,
Develop whatever beliefs you need to make sure you always attain
  your goal.

Tomorrow Never Comes_____

It's easy to procrastinate and put things off until the next day,
For many of us this becomes a habit and then it's simply our way,

"I'll do it tomorrow", we say with every good intention,
Yet instead of doing it then, we come up with another creative
    invention,

Next thing we know, tomorrow has turned into next week,
Then a month's gone by and our effort is still rather meek,

If we do this with rather unnecessary items that's just fine,
Yet it's usually some of our most important projects that get left
    behind,

Then after we've managed to let years go on by,
We find our life lacks meaning and passion and we can't figure
    out why,

We thought we'd have plenty of time to get around to that which
    was key,
Then we just lived day-to-day and let the important future plans be,

And now we wake up to find our life's almost done,
And what really mattered got caught up in tomorrow and fun,

Because tomorrow never comes, the time to do important things
    is now,
If you don't know where to start or what to do, go find out how,

Just start with a simple plan and do a little each day,
Then you'll find your life's purpose is well on its way,

Doing it tomorrow is a habit you must break,
Do it today, your future's at stake.

Ask _____

It's amazing how far we can get in this world if we only ask,
Most people are happy to help us with almost any task,

You must be kind and polite and ask in the right way,
You'll be amazed how many will help you get through your day,

If the odds are high against you and you decide you're too shy,
Your odds are absolutely zilch if you don't at least try,

Before you ask you're at nil, you have nothing to show,
You're no worse off if the answer is no,

At the same time, considering you're starting from zero,
If the answer is yes, you'll feel like a hero,

Even with high odds, the more you ask, the odds will get better,
Ask any way you have to, be it card, voice mail, or letter,

Remember, if you'll only ask, there's so much more you could gain,
If not, you'll ALWAYS wonder "what if", that's the ultimate pain.

Unexpected Pain _____

It leaves you hollow inside, as if you've been kicked hard in the gut,
It picks you up and throws you unmercifully into a deep rut,

It's unexpected pain and it hits hard and fast,
It seems as though its affects forever will last,

One day everything is going along just fine,
And the next it's as if your life's suddenly on the line,

It sneaks up and hits you when you least expect,
You try to get your guard up but you're unable to protect,

It's the toughest to endure for it hits out of the blue,
It's the most difficult pain to make it through,

For something you took for granted was taken away,
You assumed you'd always have it at the end of the day,

Now much to your chagrin that which you cherished is gone,
And somehow you must find a way to carry on,

Be thankful for what you have, for the gifts you still possess,
Then the pain of that loss will be easier to address,

For although the overwhelming pain is tough at this hour,
With time and faith you'll gain back your strength and power,

For now walk down the street and hold your head high,
There's lots of living left to do and this too will surely pass by.

LIFE = X + Y − 2 ??_____

Oh why do I have to learn this, was a thought that passed through
    my mind as a kid,
Now that I'm older, when I look back on school, I realize why they
    did what they did,

I thought, for sure twenty years from now I'll never need to have
    this knowledge,
Even if I do go onto higher education, surely I won't need this any
    further than college,

Then as I got older and found myself having to perceive many
    different situations,
It suddenly became clear why our educators came up with such
    learning creations,

They made us think differently and grasp concepts from a different
    view,
They taught us to look at many angles of a situation, both those
    head-on and askew,

In addition, thinking in different ways helped to develop our brain,
Our mind is like a muscle, in order to grow and expand, it also
    needs to train,

We learned to take that knowledge and apply it in other places,
Our learning became relative to our future life in almost all cases,

We were exposed to variety and many different areas of life's terrain,
This helped separate what interested us from that from which
    we'd rather refrain,

Yes, way back then, a lack of logic seemed to dictate the exercises
    we were given,
It is only years later that I understand the reasons by which they
    were driven,

To experience one's world completely and give us the best chance
    to thrive,
We must develop each part of our mind; we must bring every facet
    alive.

WHAT ELSE I LEARNED IN SCHOOL___

School taught me to think and develop my mind,
Yet there are many other things school also helped me find,

I learned there are times in life you must do things you don't
    want to,
Life isn't all fun and games, you also have to work in order to
    make do,

I realized much about people and relationships with others,
I learned to give and take and treat all people like sisters and
    brothers,

I faced further challenge with authority in the form of another adult,
It reinforced that if I were to break the rules, punishment would
    surely result,

I became familiar with peers and the pressure to fit in,
I learned to compete and the lessons involved should I lose or win,

It became apparent we're all in it together, striving for the same
    place,
I realized some are faster or slower when running the race,

I learned to find things in common with others, something we
    could share,
I grasped how to relate to others from different worlds, I learned
    to care,

I learned all aspects of understanding and getting along with other
    people,
I learned to work in a group and the significance of team in
    climbing the steeple,

I discovered the importance of balance and giving each area of life
    its time equal,

I found that life's a journey, not a destination, there's always a
    sequel,

Yes school taught me a great deal, years later I see,
If not for its lessons, how much worse off I'd be.

WHO DO YOU THINK YOU ARE?_____

We have all been given a gift of creativity that is ever at our
    disposal,
What we decide to create with that gift is the only questionable
    proposal,

Realize that whatever we dwell upon starts to steer us in that
    direction,
We must grab the wheel ourselves and make the course correction,

We do become what we think about, I know that much is true,
Who we are and want to become is all we really need to construe,

Just like putting food into our bodies, our mind works much the
    same,
To get the best out, we need to focus on the positives, the good
    parts of the game,

Fill your brain with stories of achievement and other inspiration,
Decide what you want, make a plan and other necessary preparation,

Then constantly visualize and think about that great person you
    want to become,
Focus with clarity and confidence, knowing any obstacles will be
    overcome,

Refuse to let negative people, stories, and activities enter your realm,
You can decide what you let in and embrace, you control the helm,

You can choose to do what most people do and take in death,
    destruction, and tragedy,
Or you can take charge of human tendency like building strong
    muscles against gravity,

We do become what we think about, our inner and outer worlds
    most often reflect,
Whatever we choose to concentrate on, is what they'll ultimately
    project.

WHY ME? _____

After a difficult day I found myself asking a typical question once
    more,
Why does my life always have to be such a difficult chore?

Can nothing come easy, I thought as I continued to feel down,
Why does every situation always seem to end in a frown?

Yet this time something was different, those thoughts passed soon,
Because something occurred to me and got me singing another tune,

As if from above a loud voice rang out in my head,
And told me of all the blessings in the life that I've led,

It told of my great family, friends, and others around me,
All my positive characteristics and traits it helped me to see,

It spoke of my health and all the opportunities that abound,
It told a story of hope and inspiration that within me could be
    found,

It reminded me of my intelligence and the bright world further on,
It expressed the years I had ahead were more than those that were
    gone,

The voice continued and it seemed as if the positives would never
    end,
At least not until I understood the message it was trying to send,

So I again asked the question "Why Me?", yet this time with a smile
    on my face,
For I realized there were many advantages to being the person who
    walked in my place,

Why am I so lucky to have all that I've got?
Why was I chosen to have such a great shot?

Why do I have such great health and great people nearby?

Why do I do so well at almost anything I try?

Why was I given so much when many others have much less?
And why have I been spared of much anxiety and stress?

Why was I given two good ears to hear and two good eyes to see?
Please someone answer me, of all the other people it could have
    been, why me?

FEAR _____

Fear is the great destroyer of all human development and progress,
It either keeps us where we are, or moves us back, either way we
    regress,

Fear is usually based in theories which are not governed by truth,
It may have been caused by one single incident found in our youth,

It makes us give up our dreams and avoid what we know we should
    do,
If you aren't careful, it will continue to grow until it completely
    engulfs you,

It sabotages anything good in our life, its destruction thorough
    and true,
It prevents you from continuing meaningful work, or seeing it
    through,

Some use fear to stop a relationship before it ever gets off the
    ground,
They wonder why no one can break through, why a soul mate
    can't be found,

Some let fear of failure stop them, for others it's fear of success,
Then just when things start going well, something stops the process,

Fear stops us from becoming more, it holds us back when we
    perform,
It scares us back into our shells, our attitude goes from hot to warm,

The greatest enemy of fear is knowledge for fear's basis is a lie,
If we choose to let fear stay, a misconception will live until we die,

The best way to destroy a fear is to learn about it then face it
    head-on,
Within a very short time, you'll be surprised, even a life phobia
    will be gone.

YOUR CALLING IN LIFE_____

As we live our lives there are many activities in which we'll take
   part,
The key is to find the one that we can take to heart,

In order to find our place in this world we must find our niche,
Or we'll carry on with a mediocre life spent stuck in a ditch,

It's important to find something we can do which we love,
An activity which inspires us to go beyond and above,

For if we can find out what that is, our life will have great meaning,
We'll have spring in our step and a positive attitude, we'll be less
   demeaning,

Start by finding something that seems to come easier than the rest,
That's probably an activity at which you can be the best,

Look at things that you've done well as the years have gone by,
Activities you've picked up easily while hardly needing to try,

Then figure out how to serve others while partaking in that task,
You'll find an answer to that question if you continue to ask,

For the people that love what they do are the ones truly wealthy,
They tend to make the most money and overall are quite healthy,

They also work harder because, to them, it's not work it's play,
They find that negatives like stress and anxiety tend to stay away,

They are happy and purposeful in each step that they take,
They are in complete control, their own destiny they make,

So if you want some passion in your life recognize their example
   and follow,
Or you'll come to the end of your life and find your uniqueness
   quite hollow,

For you can carry on aimlessly, going through the motions, prone

to depression,
Or you can discover your calling and leave this world with your
lasting impression.

THE CARROT AND THE STICK _____

We spend our entire lives either pursuing or running away,
The carrot and the stick dictate all our actions each and every day,

We gravitate toward pleasure, we move away from pain,
We use our gut to tell the difference and make our life sustain,

We don't always know why we do what we do, or move in a
   particular direction,
The choices we make aren't always clear, we make them for self-
   protection,

These two forces drive our lives, they choose our course of action,
They guide our each and every move, they drive our every
   transaction,

It's not always with the most intelligence that we have them
   guide our day,
We do have a say in the matter, we can help them choose our way,

Appreciate their guidance and what they're trying to do,
After all, it's their genuine belief they're only helping you,

Yet, realize your highest achievement they don't always serve,
They may be holding you back from all that you deserve,

You may have to make some decisions about what to focus on,
Although well-meaning, some of these defenses will be better off
   gone,

So choose which ones are protecting you and which ones hold
   you back,
And keep the ones that empower you and keep you on track.

WHAT'S REALLY IMPORTANT _____

I've seen it in older people and those close to death,
It comes with the realization that they're not full of infinite breath,

A sudden appreciation of life and what's really important,
A focus on the positive as opposed to anything even slightly
    abhorrent,

As they look back and see their life in all its infinite glory,
They now notice the most important part of the story,

The money, the fame, the toys, and riches are nice,
Yet when it comes to our souls, they don't quite suffice,

There are things people notice, that they would liked to have done,
They wish they spent less time working and more time having fun,

Suddenly promotion and the size of one's bank account isn't such
    a big deal,
The materialistic goals and petty arguments have lost most of
    their zeal,

Our days are numbered, our time on earth must come to an end,
When we get to that place it's interesting what we'll choose to
    defend,

We'll cherish the memories of special people encountered along
    the way,
For more time with them, we'd gladly cash in all our possessions
    to pay,

So learn to appreciate the little things and also those money
    can't buy,
Focus on the things that truly make your life richer, it's easy if
    you try.

ACTIONS SPEAK LOUDER THAN WORDS _____

Actions speak louder than words, it's really quite evident,
80% of us follow not by hearing, but by seeing another's precedent,

Most of us are visual, which helps to add to the legend,
Words can be misconstrued but the meaning of actions rarely bend,

We tell children and others do as I say not as I do,
Yet in the end it's our outward actions they'll ultimately construe,

We cannot set a double standard and hope it will be followed as a
rule,
Others will wonder why it's different for us; our words will face
much ridicule,

I'm sure you've seen it many times, a person saying one thing and
doing another,
They try to speak over their actions hoping their meaning we
won't uncover,

Then there are those that try to use words to explain their actions
away,
The truth's already crystal clear; they should save their breath for
another day,

Still others use words to vehemently deny an action we all know
has taken place,
If they could only hear themselves objectively, they'd realize
they're losing face,

It is true that few words are necessary when we set an example
by good action,
Our meaning will come through loud and clear much to our
satisfaction,

So keep one thing in mind when trying to set the best example,

In most cases little needs to be said, your actions are usually quite ample.

DIFFERENCES DIVIDE———————————

There's a legend throughout our society that opposites attract,
Yet what would happen if those differences had no similarities to
counteract,

When you study people and what truly brings them together,
It's actually what they have in common that keeps them with each
other forever,

As we look at differences around the world, wars over religion and
opposite belief,
It's easy to recognize that likenesses to one another is the only real
form of relief,

If you take two completely opposite people and stick them in a
place,
They'll struggle to find some common ground in almost each and
every case,

If they emerge unable to find anything the two can somewhat share,
They'll part ways, never see each other again, and not give a second
care,

Sometimes two people who are together seem opposites, this is
usually an illusion,
If we dig deeper into who they are, we'll typically draw quite a
different conclusion,

One may seem quiet, conservative, and quite impassionate in their
actions,
The other may be very outgoing, flamboyant, and full of social
interactions,

This may be a case in public where one's strength compensates
for the other,
And if you saw the two in private, there would be many similarities
to uncover,

Ultimately differences divide, while that which we have in common
    brings us together,
In any tight-knit group, what's really important to them makes them
    birds of a feather.

TRUE COLORS ─────────────────

I've heard it said many times, oh, he or she is so nice,
Yet, when someone has their back to the wall, are they really made
    of sugar and spice,

It's easy to be nice and polite when things are coming up right,
But, when someone's backed in a corner, will they laugh, run, or
    fight,

When our worlds are in turmoil and attacks come from every
    direction,
That's when our true colors emerge in the course of correction,

As we wage our defense from the weakest possible position,
To keep our heads and stay cool is a difficult proposition,

Many times we lash out and act solely on instinct,
We take lousy action and make moves much less than succinct,

Yet if we are able to keep our perspective and take a deep breath,
We'll realize things really aren't that bad, they're not life and death,

For in an instant we can take an action we'll regret for years down
    the road,
Or, we can think things through and avoid the weight of that
    emotional load,

Yes, it's in our most difficult times that character is shaped, good
    or bad,
Our actions will dictate future behavior and ultimately the life
    that we've had,

So the next time you find yourself in a difficult predicament,
Stay calm, cool, and collected, use your better judgment,

Bite your tongue, walk away, decide to do whatever it takes,
Your relationships with others will be much better, free of
    thoughtless mistakes.

ATTITUDE _____

When you look at your life and all its dimensions,
There's really one factor that determines all your intentions,

It's the one thing that can turn gray skies to blue or, blue skies to
    gray,
It's the ingredient that predicts the outcome of each and every day,

It's a thing called attitude and it's the very basis of our existence,
It'll determine whether we give up or carry on with persistence,

Unlike winning, attitude is everything AND the only thing,
Attitude either makes a situation great or makes it sting,

Our lives are made up entirely of attitude caused by emotion,
It makes our hopes small or the size of an ocean,

Attitude will dictate what you'll do in every situation,
Whether you're relaxing or involved in some confrontation,

It will affect your treatment of others and how you feel about you,
It will determine how you see your situation and carry it through,

You can affect your attitude and feelings by your own decision,
Though on some occasions you may find it a difficult proposition,

Still the choice is yours; there is always another side,
You can focus on positive or negative, the easy or tough ride,

Keep your attitude positive for it affects the outcome of your time
    here,
And whether your life is ultimately filled with misery or much
    cheer.

CAUSE AND EFFECT _____

When we look back on life and all its events,
We notice certain habits and suddenly our world makes sense,

We'll get the same result if we continue with the same action,
It's a wonder some people can't figure out their own dissatisfaction,

They've done identical things for years and each time it turns out
  the same,
They're overlooking the most important part of the game,

You have to do things differently to get a different conclusion,
This seems so elementary, yet for many, it's still an illusion,

Just as two plus two always equal four and five plus five ten,
Many other areas of our life are as predictable and will be till the
  end,

There are many laws that govern our world and what it's about,
They'll always be constants no matter how much we pout,

To tell another to learn from their mistakes is almost a cliché,
Most continue to do the same year after year and the ultimate
  price they pay,

In some cases they logically know it's wrong, yet are guided by
  feeling,
They wish to remain ignorant, even though it's their future they're
  stealing,

So realize the rule of cause and effect is the same any place,
It can work for you if it's reality you'll just decide to face,

As bad actions lead to poor results, the opposite it also true,
Changing your deeds to good will carry positive consequences
  through,

So if you don't know what to do, find a mentor, someone that's

gone before,
Either way, until you get what you want, keep changing your actions
    a little more.

THE IMPORTANCE OF GOALS _____

Most of us spend our lives moving day-to-day,
It's never even crossed our minds, there may be a better way,

There are those among us who seem to go further than the rest,
They seem to win all the time, they are prepared for any test,

They always know what they want and what they're looking for,
They seem to fear nothing and go charging through every door,

They have much inspiration, their motivation's astounding,
They are bustling with energy, their enthusiasm is abounding,

Their secret is that they've set goals from which they find drive,
And after setting a target, a greater life starts to arrive,

For without a goal there's no purpose in life, no definite direction,
We just continue doing the same things each day, there's never a
    correction,

If we refuse to set a goal, we'll always find ourselves adrift,
To give our life bearing and purpose, would be the greatest gift,

If we don't look at the bigger picture, our life is over, more or less,
If we don't get out of the daily rut, we'll fall far short of our best,

Yes, our potential is unlimited, we can have anything we desire,
Goals and a plan for their achievement is the way to start the fire,

If you're happy with being average and much less than you can be,
Then you don't need to set goals and that's the reality you'll see,

However, if you're tired of sitting on the sidelines, watching the
    world go by,
Definite, written goals will transform your life, if you'll only try,

So realize without aim and a direction, your life will not be nearly
    as grand,
A written vision and purpose will catapult your life and much
    further you'll land.

COMMENCEMENT _____

In our society we use the word commencement for graduation,
Yet we tend to view the meanings as opposites, even with our great
    education,

Most of us see graduation as a close or a conclusion,
Yet in reality it's really quite another illusion,

The word commencement actually means to begin or start,
This word is used for graduation because it's not an end, but rather,
    the first part,

The majority of us see Commencement as a goal after four years
    of drudge,
It's no wonder the word's meaning we most often smudge,

Similar words are those such as birth, dawn and creation,
Antonyms are words such as completion, end, and termination,

So instead of a finish or close we should view it as adding new vigor,
It's actually the launching pad from which our life becomes bigger,

So set Commencement and Graduation as a short-term goal not long,
If you think after that, it's all over, your viewpoint is completely
    wrong,

It should give you more life, more breath, more drive to go on,
It should be the foundation which your future is built upon,

Yes what extends before you is the genesis of a great existence,
Move forward with new enthusiasm, new vigor, and everlasting
    persistence.

ADDICTION _____

As we walk through this world there are many things to tempt us,
Not to get addicted to any is difficult, yet it's an absolute must,

Most fall victim to addiction when something isn't quite right,
They use it as a tool of escape and to avoid the internal fight,

Inside there's an issue to deal with or a hole they must fill,
Instead of facing it head on, it's easier to take a drink or a pill,

Addiction robs us of becoming the best we can be,
It makes the right answers almost impossible to see,

The first step is to realize an issue is hanging around,
The second step is to decide an answer has to be found,

The key to remember is that you're not alone in the universe,
Many others have gone before and may have even had it worse,

Turn to your family, an organized group, or a close friend,
The more people involved typically the quicker the addiction
    will end,

Knowing you have a problem is more than half of the war,
The other part is feeling its destruction down to your core,

For once you have enough pain you will find a way,
And you'll rise the very next morning to a brighter day,

Any addiction can and has been beaten I'm happy to report,
It's important to find others to lean on for some moral support,

You can beat addiction with people, hope, and enough desire,
And you'll find a much stronger person will emerge out of the fire.

FOREIGNERS _____

In my travels to foreign countries, I've realized people are all the
    same,
We just live in a separate country and speak a language of a
    different name,

For the most part we all want the same thing, happiness and peace
    of mind,
We're all searching for our place in this world, our purpose we
    hope to find,

I've heard most don't like Americans but have found the opposite
    to be true,
If you're kind, humble and nice to them, many are actually anxious
    to meet you,

You'd think the obvious differences would drown out all the rest,
But actually it's our differences that pique their interest,

For they know deep down inside we're just like them yet from a
    different place,
We're all running in the same event, it's called the human race,

So when you encounter a foreigner, treat them as one of your own,
You'll find that human bonding is much more easily sown,

For the Golden Rule is universal, treat others as you'd have them
    treat you,
Whether foreign or domestic, that's the best relationship strategy
    to pursue.

MEN VERSUS WOMEN ⎯⎯⎯⎯⎯

In studying the differences between women and men, one thing
    becomes very clear,
The ways in which they look at and interpret their worlds is
    anything but near,

Men tend to be more direct, they look head-on and charge,
Women are more indirect, instead of tunnel vision, their focus
    is large,

Men are more competitive and compare themselves to one another,
Women are more family-oriented, they think we should get along
    with each other,

Men relate more to their jobs, through it their identity they find,
Women take a more relaxed approach, they don't let work and
    image bind,

Men have a need to see completion, they need to see an end,
Women enjoy the process more, the quality of time they'll defend,

Men are more closed to other ideas, they see in black and white,
Women are open to possibilities, they'll discuss without a fight,

Men tend to be more straight on in their approach, they tend to be
    left brain,
Women see more subtleties, from close-mindedness they'll refrain,

Men are usually less sensitive, emotion they don't use much,
Women are much more tuned-in to how people feel, they possess
    a gentle touch,

Yes, men and women differ in their methods, many times to a
    great degree,
When trying to understand our different worlds, flexibility and
    an open mind are key.

Vacations _____

There comes a time in our work when we simply need a break,
A few days to unwind in the mountains or relax by a lake,

Our bodies and minds can only take so much strain,
They eventually need a holiday from the stress and pain,

That's why vacations are key to our health and well-being,
They round our lives out and give them more meaning,

For balance in all areas of our world is a critical point,
And too much of one tends to leave our souls out of joint,

You must have some down time in which you set yourself free,
It will ease the tension on your mind and make things easier to see,

Just don't over do it, too much vacation is also not good,
Listen to your gut and it will tell you when vacation you should,

Make sure you go off to somewhere well far away,
And make sure your trip is much more than a day,

And when you come back, you should be charged once again,
And this time be anxious for the hard work to begin,

A little vacation can make a once heavy load seem rather light,
And do much to set your extremely chaotic world right.

HOLIDAYS ⎯⎯⎯⎯⎯⎯⎯⎯⎯⎯⎯⎯⎯⎯⎯

Holidays are celebrations in which we all can participate,
They bring us together as we put aside indifference and hate,

Holidays remind us of the struggles of the past,
And simply what it's taken for our society to last,

They give us a time to reflect on all that is good,
And to bond with our fellow citizens through sister and
    brotherhood,

Some holidays signify major events and others represent small,
Some symbolize a time we faced evil and answered the call,

Whatever the reason, holidays give us a chance to reflect and pause,
They help us remember our obligation to our community and its
    cause,

When a holiday is upon us, remember the essence it's based upon,
Then pass along the tradition to make sure it lives on,

For without holidays, we tend to become individuals once more,
And see ourselves no more closely related than just the day before.

BIRTHDAYS _____

We celebrate one for ourselves and those close to us every year,
This event causes some to shed an occasional tear,

Yes, another Birthday is upon us, another year gone,
It's a good time to look at our life and how we're getting along,

Birthdays are special for they signify our arrival to this place,
They give us a reminder to step back to view the challenges we face,

They are an opportunity to see how far we've come,
And remember our roots and where we are from,

There are some who see a Birthday as a time to start anew,
An opportunity to think the purpose of their life through,

This is great in that it gets us to focus on what we're here for,
And hopefully even motivates us to become even more,

Birthdays should be a celebration that we're more wise and knowing,
And signify another year of mentally and emotionally growing,

For although our physical abilities may slow down a fraction,
Our wisdom and experience make us more ready for action,

So take some time on your Birthday to reflect on your past,
And maybe pick a few areas to make a positive change that will last,

Also, make sure to give thanks for what you've already got,
And the areas in which you're blessed where others are not,

Appreciate having another year of life and creation,
And welcome each Birthday with triumph and celebration.

THE IMPORTANCE OF MONEY _____

The commodity we call money plays an interesting role in our life,
Ever since the first coin was fashioned, it's been a subject of much
strife,

Many say it's the root of all evil, the devil's tool for sure,
Others believe it's mostly good, it's essence whole and pure,

The answer's probably somewhere in the middle, as opposed to
the extremes,
Depending upon how much we have tends to dictate how money
seems,

Some say money's not important, though it plays a vital role,
You'll notice this if you can't pay your debts and the stress takes
quite a toll,

It's true money can't buy happiness and at the same time, the
reverse is also true,
You'll see more people in poverty than wealth, that are miserable
through and through,

Money can however buy us nice cars, nice homes and education in
addition,
It can buy us time, fund our favorite charities, and help our social
position,

The truth is, money is a tool to use as we travel on life's path,
You'll see all the benefits and good it can do, if you'll only do the
math,

We should use it as simply a servant, a unit of exchange, to get us
where we want to go,
When we make money TOO important then we're the servant and
IT runs the show,

So remember money is important yet you must keep it in its proper
location,
And make sure you have the things money CAN'T buy and they're
in proper operation.

THE RULES OF MONEY_____

Money flows to those who know how to treat it right,
For those who don't, acquiring wealth can be quite a fight,

You have to make more money than you ultimately spend,
Or you'll always be deeper in debt in the end,

Before you pay any bills put at least ten percent away,
Or you'll find yourself in the same situation day after day,

You say expenses are twenty percent more than your take,
If that's the case, another ten percent, a difference won't make,

So always pay yourself first and all your bills after,
Or your money accounts will continue to be a disaster,

You must work for money yet it must work for you too,
You must be intelligent and think your investments through,

Educate yourself and at the same time use a financial expert,
Or away from you money will continue to divert,

Don't gamble it away, or play against high stakes,
Wealth is a long term goal, discipline it takes,

Don't be duped into letting greed cloud your vision,
Long term focus and discipline is an absolute provision,

Make sure you're not so cheap you pinch every cent,
It's a habit that even with wealth will refuse to relent,

It's also a good idea to give some money to a good cause,
It reminds us how lucky we are, it gives us some pause,

Divide your investments wisely between safety, liquidity, and yield,
And you're more than likely to stay ahead of the field,

Remember also, a happy medium is essential to attain financial

health,
Education backed by a well thought out, long term plan is the best
way to wealth.

THE STARS _____

What's really out there beyond our Earth's universe,
It's a subject on which many often converse,

We call out into space and wait for others to respond,
We send satellites and other vehicles into the great beyond,

Are we really alone or is that thought absolutely crazy,
Our theories of other life forms are nothing but hazy,

We've looked at other galaxies and have studied many stars,
Yet there's still a debate over possible life found on Mars,

If our Universe is really endless how can we be the only ones
    around,
Surely there must be some form of life that we just haven't found,

Maybe aliens are watching us and their presence they've yet to
    unveil,
Or maybe some have truly seen them yet keep that a secret detail,

So for now, we'll look up at the stars and still continue to ponder,
Is there life we're unable to see just up there over yonder,

Either way, the stars will remain the final frontier for my life's
    duration,
And we'll continue to look to them for answers of life and its
    creation.

THE WEATHER _____

Weather is an interesting phenomenon, much power it holds,
The best laid activities it either makes or it folds,

It affects people's attitudes and their general outlook on the day,
It determines what people will do, many a decision it can sway,

It spans the gambit of extremes from very pleasant to destructive
    and crude,
When we forget who's boss, it reminds us, many times with attitude,

It can shut down a part of the world and postpone any event,
Its will and desire we're helpless to prevent,

There is talk of trying to control it or using it to help mankind,
Yet a way to cage Mother Nature we're most unlikely to find,

And as we dump more into the atmosphere and our world as a
    whole,
Nature will most likely increase its fury and its destructive toll,

For we must learn to coexist with it and respect the world in which
    we live,
We have only one planet and it only has so much to give,

Weather is the weapon our planet chooses with which to fight back,
We'll be rewarded or punished based upon whether or not we keep
    things on track,

So remember, nature has the final word, it always speaks last,
It can determine if our end comes about slowly or arrives
    uncommonly fast.

MUSIC ————————————————————

Music adds color to the world in which we exist,
The powerful emotions it stirs are difficult to resist,

In movies music can make a scary scene funny or a funny one sad,
It influences whether we recall a memory as good or quite bad,

Music supplies the soundtrack to the life we have led,
We seem to get the craziest songs stuck in our head,

Music provides emotion, it can bring us up or down,
It has the power to make us sad or laugh like a clown,

Simply hearing a song can take us back to another time and place,
We find ourselves in the past and we recall an old flame's face,

Music defines generations and different civilizations in the human
race,
It can be simple or very complex depending upon individual taste,

Some say it's powerful enough to make someone take their own life,
I don't know if that's possible unless there's already a lot of strife,

But I do know that music is strong and a tool we should employ,
It can help us get in the right frame of mind for activities we enjoy,

Music can put you to sleep or give you energy to burn,
It can take a bad situation and make the negatives turn,

Decide what emotions you want to feel as you go through the day,
Then find the songs that emotionally make you feel that way,

Then when going to bed play ones that make you relax,
And when you need motivation, play those to the max,

For whatever you're after, music can aid greatly in your quest,
It will give you an emotional lift and help bring out your best.

WORK _____

Work is a necessary part of the world in which we live,
Our reward seems to be based upon the effort we give,

I've heard people say that working hard is the most important part,
However, in addition to working hard, it's also important to work
    smart,

Start with the determination to do whatever the job might ask,
Then out of all your duties, pick the most important task,

For twenty percent of your efforts will give eighty percent of
    your pay,
Stick to that most important item, even if it takes all day,

Continue on down the list until, at last, all the chores are done,
Then do a little extra before you go off and have some fun,

 It's also great to find ways to get more done in less time,
You'll find that almost any system you're able to refine,

There are usually ways to do things faster and at the same time
    better too,
There are many difficult tasks that you can learn to breeze right
    through,

Nothing that is worth it is easy, it usually takes quite a bit of drive,
Accomplishing difficult tasks will make your esteem and confidence
    thrive,

It's also important to get better at your trade, whatever it might be,
Once committed to this golden rule, higher compensation you'll
    continue to see,

Your work must also be challenging, it must force you to grow,
Or you'll find your self-development traveling ridiculously slow,

Always do more than you get paid for and work hard and smart

with ambition,
People respect hard workers and they admire intelligent ones
   in addition,

So realize we must work a bit to get the things in this world we
   desire,
Care about what you do and love it and you'll never lack the
   necessary fire.

TIME RELATIVITY_____

Time is an interesting concept when studied from afar,
It's our most valuable resource, and one in which we're all on a par,

I started to study time and notice the rules by which it goes,
I wondered why at times it passes quite slowly and at others it
    flows,

I began with the premise that time flies while we're having fun,
Then I began to dig deeper for more answers on how time is run,

Looking for reasons why time seems to vary in the speed of its
    flight,
I relived my own experiences and noticed it goes quickest at night,

Yes, surely while we're asleep is when time goes fastest,
We fall asleep and wake up to find eight hours have past us,

I wanted to know why this was true and was there anything more,
The sub-conscious runs our sleep, maybe it holds the answer in
    store,

I also noticed that the more time passes, the faster it seems to move,
It also goes by quickly when we find ourselves in a groove,

I totaled these theories with others and made a certain find,
The less conscious brain we use, the faster time seems to unwind,

Yes, as we go through life and get more and more set in our ways,
We find ourselves running into shorter and shorter days,

Unfortunately most of us live our life using very little brain,
We do the same exact thing everyday even if it's a strain,

So we walk on this earth and follow the rest of the crowd,
Only at the end do we notice the gift with which we're endowed,

So don't get caught up doing the same things in the same fashion,

You'll be robbed of your life, you'll end up with no passion,

Use your conscious brain, step out of that thoughtless trend,
Or you'll find your life boring and uneventful right to the end.

Be Unreasonable in
What You Expect _____

Those in our society who have achieved anything great,
Have never been happy just carrying their own weight,

They have not been reasonable in what they expect,
A positive attitude and unmatched desire they often project,

For they realize that one person CAN change the world,
What hasn't been accomplished is just a plan not yet unfurled,

They believe things can be done that others dare not dream,
They persist in their vision no matter how crazy it may seem,

They believe in themselves and breaking their previous best,
They focus completely on their goal, they disregard the rest,

They don't think about limits or what hasn't been done,
They pursue even life-threatening feats and treat them as fun,

As far as what others may say, they really don't worry,
They decide on an action and get after it in a hurry,

Yes, you must be unreasonable to change things as they are,
In this world it's the only way you'll get very far,

Chart a course as if you have no limits and watch most of them fall,
And when challenges and obstacles try to stop you, answer the call,

You can have ANYTHING you want, you are a limitless being,
Nothing can stop you from fulfilling what your inner mind's seeing.

SECTION 2

THE PEOPLE IN OUR LIVES

Happy Mother's Day _____

Moms are very unique in the world which we live,
They never want anything except more opportunities to give,

When as babies we cry in the night, they always come to the rescue,
They're always there for us, they never miss their cue,

No matter what, they love us for who we are,
When we need their help, their presence is never far,

We're their first thought before bed and also upon waking,
It's our favorite foods that they're most often making,

They teach us proper language, grammar, and punctuation too,
When we start a project, they're there to make sure we carry it
    through,

They make sure we watch our manners and play well with others,
They make certain we get along with our sisters and brothers,

They constantly think about us and are concerned for our
    well-being,
When they think of our life down the road, a bright future
    they're seeing,

They watch many baseball games and even go to our school play,
It's not uncommon for them to also end up in the PTA,

They send us to school well-fed and well-dressed,
They make sure we have all we need and that we're always blessed,

You're always their baby, even when you're turning gray and
    getting old,
When they made your Mom, they definitely broke the mold,

Yes, like Dads, Moms put us before them in all that they do,
They love us completely, through and through,

Yes a Mom's love is unconditional, it's there no matter what,
She doesn't always have to say it, we know in our gut,

A Mom is the personification of tireless dedication and love,
Thank your lucky stars for her, she's definitely a gift from above.

HAPPY FATHER'S DAY _____

As I sat down to describe Dads in all their infinite glory,
I realized our biological beginning is only part of the story,

For a Dad is more than the contributor of half our DNA,
He's a force that is with us nearly every day,

His part in conception is the least important part of the equation,
The critical factor is his influence in our after birth creation,

He changes a diaper or two, our first words he helps us find,
When we take our first step, he's not far behind,

He teaches us to ride a bike and eventually to drive,
It's his years of experience and advice on which we thrive,

He sometimes disciplines us and puts us back into line,
When we think our world's devastated, he lets us know all will
    be fine,

He's a role model to follow, we learn his values and virtue,
He shows us the way, his actions always speak true,

He's a pillar of support, someone we can go to in any event,
He's someone that will listen when we simply need to vent,

He prepares us to tackle the world and fly from the nest,
No matter what happens, he thinks we're the best,

He's there to call on even when we think we're all grown,
His words still carry that comforting tone,

He'll forever be part of us even after he's gone,
His strength exists within us, his spirit lives on,

Yes, the man we call Dad spends years putting his interests after us,
Out of love, he sees his total sacrifice for us an absolute must,

What makes him a Father is years of being there through the good

and the bad,
Yes, total dedication, devotion, and sacrifice is what makes a Dad.

GRANDPARENTS _____

Grandparents are very special in many different ways,
Their endless supply of smiles and hugs brightens many days,

They get to miss most difficulties of parenting and focus on the fun,
Though they love to look after either their Granddaughter or
    Grandson,

They're in a different role this time, now they get to spoil,
They focus on the pleasant parts, they avoid most of the toil,

When children get to see them, it's a special gift,
It's almost always a joyous occasion with rarely any rift,

Grandparents entertain with their stories, both those of truth
    and lore,
And as the children grow, they begin to appreciate them more,

Yes, Grandparents portray the joy and good this world can represent,
Both Grandparents and Grandchildren think the other is Heaven
    sent,

Grandparents are a significant part of who we are and who we
    hope to be,
The moment we finally realize this, their true importance is
    easy to see,

For they are the gateway to our future and the story of years
    gone by,
Listen to them carefully and learn all you can, it's easy if you try,

Keep the connection with your Grandparents strong and true,
    don't ever let it fray,
But most importantly, appreciate them for the great blessing
    they portray.

BROTHERS AND SISTERS _____

Our siblings are among the first people we encounter in the world,
They've gone before us, so they help us get things unfurled,

Sometimes there's jealousy and competition ensues,
Yet when we get hurt, they usually help fix a bump or a bruise,

Sibling rivalry is the first place we learn to fight,
Then we reach a certain age and we start to see the light,

Because though brothers and sisters are usually a unique bunch,
As we get older they're the ones we can count on in a crunch,

Blood's thicker than water, so the saying goes,
Siblings usually rush to our side when we encounter foes,

They feel the bond of family which was created by birth,
They realize the family relationship helps guide their self-worth,

For it's on the frame of family relations that others are ground,
If we get along with family, other good relationships are easily
    found,

Our siblings also realize that we are most similar to them,
It's from this understanding that strong relationships stem,

So love your brothers and sisters and their lives and reputations
    defend,
Because you're all in it together, you're family until the end.

FAMILY _____

When you look at a society from its earliest creation,
You'll find that families make up its basic foundation,

The family consists of those closely related by blood,
The purpose is to flood each other with love,

The relationship with your family sets the framework for the
    rest of your life,
It tends to dictate whether other associations will be smooth
    or have strife,

Typically the apple doesn't fall far from the tree,
Yet if you look just a little, many examples you'll see,

For people with a bad upbringing take it in one of two directions,
They use it for an excuse, or a reason to make some corrections,

No matter how you were brought up, the decisions your own,
You decide what actions and behaviors you'll ultimately condone,

You don't choose your family, but you choose how you exist,
Whether good or bad, you'll decide if your family values persist,

You learn how to live from your family, that much is true,
Still your eventual future, you'll need to construe,

Make sure to build a strong foundation of trust and love,
Don't give up when things get tough and push comes to shove,

Also realize you can help with some insight or guiding provisions,
Yet ultimately you must let family members make their own
    decisions,

Be there for support and to pick them up when they fall,
Be there for encouragement and to help them give it their all,

For we're in this together, we're all part of the same clan,
A strong and happy family is the most important part of the plan.

FRIENDS ⸻⸻⸻⸻⸻⸻⸻

A friend is someone who is always there,
A friend will listen when you need someone to care,

They take us for who we are and don't try to change us,
In a pinch they are people we can always trust,

When we ask their opinion, they'll tell us the truth,
They'll let us know if we're acting crazy and without any couth,

Friends stick by us both in thick and thin,
They help us straighten our world when it's in a tailspin,

They're someone you can call at three in the morning,
When you hang out with them, it's rarely boring,

They'll stand up and fight for you with every last breath,
You swear you'll be friends at least until death,

You can sit with a friend for hours and say nothing at all,
And come away from the experience insisting you had a ball,

You can tell them a secret and know it won't go anywhere,
If you'd like to sit down, they'll gladly give up their chair,

A good friendship is balanced between give and take,
It takes work and it's a commitment both people must make,

When a friendship is strong, you feel it deep inside,
It's a connection with another, in which you take great pride,

So cherish your friends and work on keeping that link strong,
With an abundance of close friends you'll never go wrong.

MENTORS _____

Mentors are an important part of the world in which we live,
They pass on the life experience and knowledge they have to give,

They're around to make sure we don't reinvent the wheel,
When we have perplexing questions, the answers they reveal,

A mentor is someone that's already traveled down our direction,
For almost any circumstance, they at least have a suggestion,

In addition to a professional, they're many times a friend,
They'll stand by us on projects up until the bitter end,

Mentors are critical for they help guide our way,
They make sure the proper path is where we stay,

They also pass on tradition and tricks of the vocation,
They've seen virtually every scenario and situation,

Yes, mentors are key in helping professions live on,
Without them the lessons of the past would be gone,

If you have a mentor, let them how much you appreciate them,
And realize it's from their help that your success does stem,

Then challenge yourself to be someone's mentor now or down
   the road,
The immense satisfaction will be worth the small additional
   work load.

SEASONED CITIZENS _____

There's an interesting occurrence as we move on in age,
Our increasing knowledge transforms us into a wise person or sage,

It's true as we become older, in certain areas, the better we get,
As we move on in years, over unimportant things we no longer fret,

As more time passes we begin to realize what's important and
essential,
We gain more experience and increase our already amazing
potential,

The aged among us have an incredible wealth of experience
and knowledge,
Surely more real than you'll find in any university or college,

They have quite a story to tell, of history first hand,
They lived through the Wars and Germany's last stand,

They can teach us about our heritage and our culture too,
They can tell us what's myth from that which is true,

They make sure we're reminded of the mistakes of the past,
They tell us stories to make sure the vivid images last,

Yes, our Senior Citizens and their memories are treasures to be
cherished,
Without their sacrifice, our world would surely have perished,

Learn from them, ask questions, they're dying to tell,
The experiences of their lives, both the heaven and hell,

For once they leave this world, their wealth of information is gone,
Yet if you've listened to them, through you it lives on,

So appreciate our Seasoned Population and all they have to give,
And a much more rewarding life we're all sure to live.

PETS _____

Pets can be an important part of the world in which we live,
If we simply let one in our life, there are many benefits they
    can give,

People with pets have been found to be more at ease,
They suffer from fewer illnesses and also less disease,

Pets can teach children how to deal with many a situation,
Pets can help in their emotional growth and aid in their creation,

Pets provide company for people who have no one around,
In your pet a best friend can always be found,

When we need them with us, they're always there,
When we feel a bit down they seem like they care,

Their love does not come to us with any conditions,
They're included in holidays and family traditions,

They don't mind if the weather outside is good or bad,
They love us regardless of the day that we've had,

When we come home they always greet us with joy,
They're not always making demands or asking for a new toy,

Yet we don't only need them, they need us too,
Their over abundance is a fact that's painfully true,

So if you don't have a pet, get one to brighten your day,
And a lifetime of devotion and gratitude they'll happily pay.

SECTION 3 ⸺

LIVING WITH THE PEOPLE IN OUR LIVES

GETTING TO KNOW YOU—
KEEPING THE FIRE _____

The behavior is pre-history, it's the game that's lasted ages,
It is one that's been quite baffling both to wise men and to sages,

It's the actions of men and women and the fashion in which
    they love,
Initially on their best behavior, any bad actions they rise above,

They both are very cognizant of how they look and also what
    they wear,
They'll do nearly anything to convince the other they're a
    perfect pair,

The man brings flowers and candy and always opens up her door,
He's careful not to drink too much and go sprawling to the floor,

She in turn looks good for him and makes sure each hair's in place,
She makes sure all her makeup's right and she presents a pleasant
    face,

They both make an effort to stay in shape and watch the things
    they eat,
They thoroughly enjoy each other's company, togetherness is a treat,

As they find out about each other, every new facet is a delight,
They seem to admire each quality, there's rarely a reason to fight,

Then once they fall in love and are committed, some seem to
    forget why,
While others continue to adore each other, they strengthen that
    loving tie,

Start each day by thanking the heavens you met and that your
    paths intersected,
Remember what you love about each other and get your relationship
    resurrected,

The secret to loving each other forever is to focus on the others
    best,
Compliment them, appreciate them, and throw out all the rest,

Tell them how lucky you are to have them, your world is truly
    blessed,
Your goodwill will return to you, even more than you might have
    guessed,

Make sure you empathize with them and listen to them talk about
    their day,
Respect their feelings and opinions, it's the highest compliment you
    can pay,

Bring home flowers, give them cards, and do unique things for no
    special affair,
Finally, tell and show them how much you love them and how much
    you really care.

Random Acts of Kindness _____

It's funny how we can affect each other through the simplest of
    our actions,
A basic facial expression or gesture can get the most overwhelming
    of reactions,

Try being nice to others and walk through your day with a smile,
When helping out friends and family, go the extra mile,

Compliment those with whom you're employed and tell them they
    do good work,
For those that tend to bother you, decide to focus on a positive
    quirk,

Treat a stranger as a friend and help them find their way,
You'll find that assisting others tends to brighten up your day,

Give to charities, volunteer and expect nothing in return,
Give completely of yourself, don't let time or money be a concern,

You'll feel more a part of your world, your self esteem will rise,
You'll find your world miraculously changing much to your surprise,

For the positives will build up and come back to you at least
    ten-fold or more,
While at the same time negatives and bad memories will walk
    out the door,

For the world revolves around people, through them most
    happiness you will find,
Yet if your relationships are lacking, you'll discover your world
    is quite unkind,

So wave to people, say hello and don't wait for them to make the
    first move,
Once you make a habit of this, you'll soon be in the groove,

Practice random acts of kindness and watch the reactions that
  evolve,
You'll soon find peace and happiness about your world revolve.

HOW TO TREAT OTHERS _____

Treat others as you would have them treat you,
The saying is old, yet it's still absolutely true,

There are several important aspects of how people are,
If you remember these and use them you'll travel quite far,

The first is that people like to stand out more than the rest,
They like recognition and affirmation that they're the best,

They like to tell their story and want us to listen with both ears,
They want us to empathize with their heartache and tears,

They desire to be accepted as they are and be part of a group,
They want to be brought up-to-date and kept in the loop,

As human beings we all have needs we strive to fulfill,
If we can all work together we'll be better off still,

Treat another as if they are the most important in the universe,
Focus on them, not yourself, when you two should converse,

Look them in the eye with interest, don't turn away,
Empathize with them and their difficult day,

Accept them completely for who they are and throw the rest aside,
Let them know you're concerned and someone in which they can
    confide,

And if you ever find your relations with others getting off track,
There's only one thought you need hold to get those special bonds
    back,

Treating others with kindness and compassion should be your only
    concern,
For you'll find that the actions you show others are actions they'll
    return.

RELATIONSHIPS _____

Any good relationship takes its share of work,
Yet the tendency to be lazy is a funny human quirk,

Some go into marriage thinking the effort will be all downhill,
Then when they see the work involved, their vows they can't fulfill,

Another challenge is selfishness in which we sometimes partake,
To let it into too much of our life is the ultimate mistake,

We'll sometimes fight, sometimes argue, and sometimes
    misunderstand,
The test is when the other needs us, do we always lend a
    helping hand,

At times we must give more than we take and occasionally the
    opposite is true,
Overall it must be fairly equal to carry the relationship through,

It's true romantic relationships take more effort than that of friends,
Yet with too little work in either, the connection eventually ends,

Sometimes it's easy to lose touch while living our busy life,
Lack of contact can end a relationship just the same as some sort
    of strife,

We need to keep the goal in mind, ultimate connection with
    another being,
If we keep our focus on the other person, that's what we'll soon
    be seeing,

Remember, relationships take time and effort yet the finest
    prize is worth a ton,
Such a connection with another being that you both truly
    feel as one.

THE HUMAN RACE _____

Something occurred to me as I traveled the other day,
People in other cars were all going the same way,

Not just the ones going the same direction as me,
Even those coming at me from as far as the eye could see,

I realized ultimately we're all going to the same place,
We're all part of this thing called the human race,

As we go through our days we chase the same plan,
That's to get ourselves to the promised land,

We all have a different idea of what should be the perfect vision,
Our values and beliefs are based upon that ultimate decision,

There are millions of different ways there and many roads to take,
We do the best with what we have, our history we make,

Some of us are still trying to figure out exactly what we desire,
We're still looking for that motivation, we're still searching for
      that fire,

Maybe we could get together and help each other make it through,
The fact that many heads are better than one is definitely true,

And if we all pulled together, I'm sure easier it would seem,
We'd get more accomplished faster working as a team,

So get a good group of people that you can definitely trust,
Share the dreams and visions found in each of us,

Then support each other and help each member get where they
      need to go,
Remember we're all in it together, we're all part of the same show.

HELPING OTHERS

One fact that remains from the day of our birth until we die,
Is that there are many others around us also trying to get by,

There are unlimited opportunities to help others along the way,
There are many means to brighten almost anyone's day,

There are many less fortunate who could use our aid,
Yet we must watch how extensively that helpful plan's laid,

For it is possible to help another more than we should,
And we end up doing things that they probably could,

For when we help too much we further disable,
Yet when we help just enough then we enable,

When we assist others we should also teach them something new,
Perhaps a survival strategy that could carry them through,

Like the person who eats for a day when a fish is given to them,
Or the person taught to fish from which a great skill does stem,

There are some among us that need lots of help and total dedication,
Then there are others that just need a little help or a
    recommendation,

The trick is to know the difference and help just enough,
Or you'll make their road increasingly tough,

To want to help and take action is an excellent start,
When it comes right down to it, that's the most important part,

Just use your best judgment and do the best that you can,
Helping each other is the most important part of the plan.

DEALING WITH PEOPLE
YOU DON'T WANT TO _____

At times in our lives we'll come into contact with those we
    don't prefer,
Yet the right thing to do is to be courteous and not cause a stir,

It could be some family members, neighbors, or old friends,
Just be cautious of the message your interaction sends,

You don't need to be overly friendly yet visibly upset is not best,
Just concentrate on being moderately pleasant and forget all the rest,

By being mean-spirited you have absolutely nothing to gain,
In fact, considering what else you could lose is the reason to refrain,

Most people cringe when they see negative situations and
    interactions,
You're likely to cause more problems with more people with
    negative actions,

People admire those who can rise above and take the high road,
And you'll feel much better knowing your best side you showed,

For you'll realize that the problem is not within you,
You are a bigger person and you've shown higher virtue,

The same rules apply if you are confronted by someone,
Stay calm and collected and you'll find a moral victory you've won,

For the other person will seem like someone not quite sane,
And you'll walk away having the better name,

Remember by acting negatively with others you can go nowhere
    but down,
You'll gather much more positive attention with a smile than
    a frown.

You Light Up My Life _____

There are people in our lives that help make our world bright,
When we're confused, or down, they pick us up and set things right,

We sometimes just assume that they'll always be there,
Even though taking them for granted is really unfair,

We don't want to picture a day when they'll actually be gone,
Yet that reality is present and one day it will dawn,

We must let others know we appreciate them and what they do
    for us,
We must let them know they're important and have our
    ultimate trust,

We may think they see what they mean to us, however, that
    may not be so,
Only the actual words followed by action will truly let them know,

So show those important in your life how much they mean to you,
Don't wait until it's too late when either one of your lives is
    through,

At each meeting treat them as if it's the last time you'll speak,
See them as a very important person, one that's extremely unique,

Focus on the present and how much their company you enjoy,
Let them know how you feel, there's no need to be coy.

PEOPLE = LIFE'S
SIGNIFICANT EVENTS _____

When you look back on life and its victories, as well as trials and
   tribulations,
Take a gaze at the people and causes that participated in those
   situations,

In the majority of cases you'll find people have been heavily
   involved,
People are the factor around which our most significant events
   revolved,

I've heard the number is as low as 70 or as high as 80 to 90 percent,
Looking at my own life, I've seen people in almost every event,

Whether happiness or pain, other people usually play a significant
   part,
People are almost always involved in the most critical matters of
   the heart,

So realize just how important communicating and getting along
   with others can be,
Our lives and relationships tend to be much better when with
   open eyes we see,

Keep an open mind, treat others kindly and try to see their
   point of view,
Or else you'll find life's exciting experiences somewhere
   between none and few.

PARENTING _____

Of all the jobs a person can have, one's more important than
the rest,
It requires that we're always on call, it demands nothing but
our best,

With this job comes huge responsibility and patience is a most
important trait,
It leaves little room for mistakes and requires you to practice
much restraint,

It's simply all or nothing, a total commitment you must make,
It's a lifetime requirement, vacations from it you can't take,

The job is that of a parent and it requires us to be all that we can be,
For it's not only our own lives now, it's also our children's you see,

It's necessary to put the needs of your children before those of
your own,
Make sure to set a good example, your children will reap what
you have sown,

You must give nothing short of everything and expect absolutely
nothing back,
If you give your children any less, there are many things they'll
surely lack,

For your children are dependant upon you to give them a good
foundation,
You must bring out the best in your values and beliefs to aid in
their creation,

It's essential to help them become all they can and keep their
attitude pure,
They'll reflect simply what they learn from you, of that much
you can be sure,

Parenting is the most important job in the world, it's a blessing to
 receive the call,
Lead by example, love your children unconditionally and
 give it nothing but your all.

SECTION 4

A FEW SHORT ESSAYS

PLAYERS VERSUS SPECTATORS_____

For the most part, the majority of our lives are spent either PARTICI-
PATING in the game of life or WATCHING others participate in the
game of life. You are either a player or a spectator.

You're either busy watching TV. and seeing how other people live
or, you're busy living.

You're either listening to songs on the radio and radio talk
shows or, you're listening to educational tapes and C.D.s and getting
educated.

You've either launched your ship and you're out looking for new
adventures and dragons to slay or, you're on the shoreline watching
or, waiting for your ship to come in.

You're either on the field of play or, you're in the stands.

You're either in awe of those around you or, you're working on
becoming awesome.

You're either a leader or, a follower.

You're either setting the standard or, you're following one.

All of us spend some time in both areas. We need to. That's what
gives our life balance. Even the greatest of athletes aren't ALWAYS
participating, they watch great sporting events also. However, the area
where you spend the majority of your life will dictate what kind of life
you're likely to have.

When you look at people that have truly had full lives, that have
been participants, you'll see that they've participated throughout their
entire lives. Even people, such as athletes, whose careers in their
original chosen field can be relatively short, find new adventures and
conquests once they've retired from their original career. They stay
involved in the game of life, striving to become more than they were
the day before.

The choice is yours. No one else that has ever walked this planet
has been exactly like you and no one ever will be. You ARE an
original. You can choose to go through this life an original, a player,
and you can die an original. On the other hand, you can watch and
follow everyone else, satisfied with just getting by, satisfied with just
good enough, settling for second best, leaving no legacy, and you can
die being one of the sheep.

WHY WORRY _____

People's worries basically fall into one of two categories, those they can do something about and those they can't do anything about.

To worry about the things you can't do anything about makes no sense because, either way, the event is going to carry itself out unaffected by what you do or don't do. Worrying serves no purpose because it will not affect the outcome. At the same time, worry will put you in a worse position due to the stress caused by negative emotions. You may lose sleep, you may have trouble eating, or, you may eat more, usually which ever is the worst case scenario for you. And for what? For absolutely nothing. In the end no matter how much you've worried, the outcome will be exactly the same.

To worry about things you can control also makes no sense. A more productive course of action is to get busy affecting and controlling the outcome, steering it in a positive direction. If you are taking positive action and doing all that you can, it's impossible to worry because a negative and positive thought cannot occupy your mind at the same time. Even in the situations you can control however, there comes a point when you've done all that you can do. Look at the situation, evaluate it and do all that is REASONABLY possible to either encourage a positive outcome or prevent a negative one. Then let the chips fall where they may with the peace of mind that you have done your part.

Winners never worry because they realize that worrying never brings about a positive result. Worry is a negative emotion which saps your strength and energy. It is not productive, it is counterproductive. Worrying only causes second guessing, stress and anxiety, none of which are good. Winners pro-actively plan, anticipate, prepare, take action, then when they've done all that they can, they remove the weight from their shoulders and let life unfold before them with confidence and peace of mind that all will work out for the best.

LIFE EQUALS CHOICE _____

Our whole life is a choice. Every conscious waking second of each and every day is a choice. It's a choice about what to focus on. It's a choice about how to feel. It's a choice about how to react and it's a choice about what direction our life will ultimately go in.

Each second we're deciding what's important to us, what we're going to make a priority. These decisions are based upon who we think we are, what we think our capabilities are, and what we think we want for ourselves, as well as, what we think others want for us or from us.

It may seem quite basic and even a little difficult to believe, however, every emotion you feel, every action you take, every thought that passes through your brain is a decision at some level. Sure, many emotions and thoughts may seem automatic. This is because we have learned them and they have become habitual. They may spill forward without you needing to even think about them, however, ultimately what is happening is your brain sees, hears, or feels this stimulus and asks, "What does this mean to me?", then acts accordingly. You can make a conscious choice to change these habitual reactions.

You start by deciding you can make up your mind to be happy or upset. You can decide to focus on what's right in your life or, you can focus on what's wrong. You can remember pleasant experiences from your past or painful ones. You can dread difficult situations you're sure to face or, you can look forward to upcoming adventures and challenges.

Even unpleasant experiences are helped by good choices or, made worse by bad ones. A flat tire is still flat whether you're the happiest person the world or, the most miserable. However, although the experience may not be better with a great attitude, it will definitely be worse with a poor one.

The choice of the attitude you have affects every aspect of your life. If you choose to focus on the positive instead of the negative, you will automatically attract more positive, up-beat people and situations which will lead to a more positive up-beat life. At the same time, you will repel negative people and situations.

The truth is, you won't always win. Occasionally things will go wrong. Yet, if you decide to have a positive, healthy attitude ahead of time, the bad times won't be as bad and they won't last as long. You'll also find yourself experiencing more of the good times and they will be more intense. Also, if you embed the decision to be positive and upbeat no matter what, you'll find the negative emotions and reactions, that at one time seemed "automatic", won't be automatic anymore and they'll fade away.

When you wake up in the morning, don't let things just hit you unconsciously deciding how to feel and react. Instead consciously decide what to focus on and how to feel. Concentrate on the good parts of your life. The parts that make you happy or inspire you. Whether or not you do this, the day will unfold before you either way. The sun will rise in the East and set in the West. The weather patterns will continue to flow regardless of how you choose to live. Wouldn't it be nice to decide to have a good day no matter what? Wouldn't it be nice to be positive and attract positive people and positive situations? Wouldn't it be nice to look at events in your life in a way that builds you up instead of breaks you down? Wouldn't it be nice to decide a failed attempt is simply a learning experience? And wouldn't it be nice to use a negative word from another to give you more drive and determination?

This may sound a little far-fetched or, perhaps too good to be true, however, it is true. Once you accept that you ALWAYS have a choice and you COMPLETELY CONTROL your thoughts, your whole life will change and the light will finally go on.

You do decide what kind of day, month, year, and life you'll ultimately have. You decide when you'll no longer settle for second best and you decide when to make a stand and change your life. You decide who has power over you. You decide whether to put yourself in a situation, stay in a situation, or leave a situation. You decide what emotions to feel and whether you'll let them overwhelm you or stop them in their tracks. You decide what to put into your body physically, mentally, spiritually and you decide what comes out.

It's your life and your decision. If you don't like where you are, or where you're going, change it. If you think there's more inside of you that needs to be brought out and explored, make a conscious decision and act on it. Go forth and choose to live a happy, fulfilling and joyous life.

DREAMS _____

Dreams—not the ones we have at night while we sleep, but the real ones. Where you want your life to go, what you want to become, what you hope for those around you.

More than goals written on a piece of paper, dreams are visions. Dreams are inspirations. They are a culmination of our highest hopes and best-case scenarios. They show us in our perfect light, the best we can possibly be. We envision the world a better place, where we have made a difference. Where our contribution is significant to us, be it on a level that has a profound influence on the lives of many others or, perhaps, only a few.

Our dreams are many. Sometimes they are not always as clear as we'd like, but in the end they are all the same. To leave this world a better place than when we arrived.

Our dreams are our own. They are individual, significant, and sometimes very personal. As others enter our lives, some of them are blessed in that they become special enough to be woven into those dreams. When we share our dreams with others, it's more than just a sharing of this world though, it's a sharing of our souls.

As we weave others into our dreams and our lives, most of the time we are unaware of just how deeply we've done so. It is only in the moments of extreme joy or pain, of one of those blessed, that it becomes clear that they are one of our special few. As they breathe, we breathe, as they live, we live, as they cheer, we cheer, and as they hurt, we hurt.

During my life I've felt both the joy of another's dream coming true and the pain of another's dream ending. Truly sharing in another's joy is special, however, the significance of the painful emotions associated with the ending of another's dream was also quite special. For it signified such a bonding with another being that their dreams had also become my dreams. Our souls had become one.

The sharing of dreams with others leads back to the rule which I now realize is the gateway to truly understanding another, truly bonding with another: Respect others, appreciate others, try to see their point of view and most importantly, treat others as you would have them treat you.

It is in our greatest moments of victory and defeat that our dreams are either realized or reshaped. Some people, through defeat, lose their dreams all together. No matter how devastating though, we must find a way to carry on. All of us have been beaten from time to time. All of us have misstepped or done things of which we are not proud. Anyone who's lived any kind of life has experienced the human frailty of being temporarily defeated or making mistakes. That's part of what life is all about. For without the bad times, we would not be able to fully appreciate the good ones.

God only knows what our future holds, however, those blessed few are forever a part of us now, because we have shared dreams and love. We have shared souls.

Yes, the sun will rise tomorrow and the day after that and the world will continue with or without us. I will be eternally grateful that I have been lucky enough to share another's dreams and truly become part of another being, part of another soul, for such is the essence of life and having truly lived. And on the day that the sun rises to find me no longer here, all I can ask is that my dreams live on to touch and inspire as many people as humanly possible.

John James Chapin